LifeChange

A NAVPRESS BIBLE STUDY SERIES

A life-changing
encounter with God's Word

PHILIPPIANS

Find peace and contentment
in perilous times.

D0012151

NAVPRESS

A NavPress resource published in alliance
with Tyndale House Publishers, Inc.

NAVPRESS⬤

NavPress is the publishing ministry of The Navigators, an international Christian organization and leader in personal spiritual development. NavPress is committed to helping people grow spiritually and enjoy lives of meaning and hope through personal and group resources that are biblically rooted, culturally relevant, and highly practical.

For more information, visit www.NavPress.com.

For information about special discounts for bulk purchases, please contact Tyndale House Publishers at csresponse@tyndale.com, or call 1-800-323-9400.

ISBN 978-0-89109-072-4

Printed in the United States of America

24 23 22 21 20 19
37 36 35 34 33 32

CONTENTS

ACKNOWLEDGMENTS

The LIFECHANGE series has been produced through the coordinated efforts of a team of Navigator Bible study developers and NavPress editorial staff, along with a nationwide network of field-testers.

SERIES EDITOR: KAREN LEE-THORP

HOW TO USE THIS STUDY

Objectives

Most guides in the LifeChange series of Bible studies cover one book of the Bible. Although the LifeChange guides vary with the books they explore, they share some common goals:

1. To provide you with a firm foundation of understanding and a thirst to return to the book.

2. To teach you by example how to study a book of the Bible without structured guides.

3. To give you all the historical background, word definitions, and explanatory notes you need, so that your only other reference is the Bible.

4. To help you grasp the message of the book as a whole.

5. To teach you how to let God's Word transform you into Christ's image.

Each lesson in this study is designed to take sixty to ninety minutes to complete on your own. The guide is based on the assumption that you are completing one lesson per week, but if time is limited you can do half a lesson per week or whatever amount allows you to be thorough.

Flexibility

LifeChange guides are flexible, allowing you to adjust the quantity and depth of your study to meet your individual needs. The guide offers many optional questions in addition to the regular numbered questions. The optional questions, which appear in the margins of the study pages, include the following:

Optional Application. Nearly all application questions are optional; we hope you will do as many as you can without overcommitting yourself.

For Thought and Discussion. Beginning Bible students should be able to handle these, but even advanced students need to think about them. These questions frequently deal with ethical issues and other biblical principles. They often offer cross-references to spark thought, but the references do not give obvious answers. They are good for group discussions.

For Further Study. These include: (a) cross-references that shed light on a topic the book discusses, and (b) questions that delve deeper into the passage. You can omit them to shorten a lesson without missing a major point of the passage.

If you are meeting in a group, decide together which optional questions to prepare for each lesson, and how much of the lesson you will cover at the next meeting. Normally, the group leader should make this decision, but you might let each member choose his or her own application questions.

As you grow in your walk with God, you will find the LIFECHANGE guide growing with you—a helpful reference on a topic, a continuing challenge for application, a source of questions for many levels of growth.

Overview and details

The study begins with an overview of Philippians. The key to interpretation is context—what is the whole passage or book *about?*—and the key to context is purpose—what is the author's *aim* for the whole work? In lesson 1 you will lay the foundation for your study of Philippians by asking yourself, "Why did the author (and God) write the book? What did they want to accomplish? What is the book about?"

In lessons 2 through 10, you will analyze successive passages of Philippians in detail. Thinking about how a paragraph fits into the overall goal of the book will help you to see its purpose. Its purpose will help you see its meaning. Frequently reviewing a chart or outline of the book will enable you to make these connections.

In lesson 11, you will review Philippians, returning to the big picture to see whether your view of it has changed after closer study. Review will also strengthen your grasp of major issues and give you an idea of how you have grown from your study.

Kinds of questions

Bible study on your own—without a structured guide—follows a progression. First you observe: What does the passage *say?* Then you interpret: What does the passage *mean?* Lastly you apply: How does this truth *affect* my life?

Some of the "how" and "why" questions will take some creative thinking, even prayer, to answer. Some are opinion questions without clear-cut right answers; these will lend themselves to discussions and side studies.

Don't let your study become an exercise in knowledge alone. Treat the passage as God's Word, and stay in dialogue with Him as you study. Pray,

"Lord, what do You want me to see here?" "Father, why is this true?" "Lord, how does this apply to my life?"

It is important that you write down your answers. The act of writing clarifies your thinking and helps you to remember.

Study aids

A list of reference materials, including a few notes of explanation to help you make good use of them, begins on page 111. This guide is designed to include enough background to let you interpret with just your Bible and the guide. Still, if you want more information on a subject or want to study a book on your own, try the references listed.

Scripture versions

Unless otherwise indicated, the Bible quotations in this guide are from the New International Version of the Bible. Other versions cited are the Revised Standard Version Bible (RSV), the New American Standard Bible (NASB), and the King James Version (KJV).

Use any translation you like for study, preferably more than one. A paraphrase such as The Living Bible is not accurate enough for study, but it can be helpful for comparison or devotional reading.

Memorizing and meditating

A psalmist wrote, "I have hidden your word in my heart that I might not sin against you" (Psalm 119:11). If you write down a verse or passage that challenges or encourages you and reflect on it often for a week or more, you will find it beginning to affect your motives and actions. We forget quickly what we read once; we remember what we ponder.

When you find a significant verse or passage, you might copy it onto a card to keep with you. Set aside five minutes during each day just to think about what the passage might mean in your life. Recite it over to yourself, exploring its meaning. Then, return to your passage as often as you can during your day, for a brief review. You will soon find it coming to mind spontaneously.

For group study

A group of four to ten people allows the richest discussions, but you can adapt this guide for other sized groups. It will suit a wide range of group types, such as home Bible studies, growth groups, youth groups, and businessmen's studies. Both new and experienced Bible students, and new and mature Christians, will benefit from the guide. You can omit or leave for later years any questions you find too easy or too hard.

The guide is intended to lead a group through one lesson per week. However, feel free to split lessons if you want to discuss them more thoroughly. Or, omit some questions in a lesson if preparation or discussion time is limited. You can always return to this guide for personal study later. You will be able to discuss only a few questions at length, so choose some for discussion and others for background. Make time at each discussion for members to ask about anything they didn't understand.

Each lesson in the guide ends with a section called "For the group." These sections give advice on how to focus a discussion, how you might apply the lesson in your group, how you might shorten a lesson, and so on. The group leader should read each "For the group" at least a week ahead so that he or she can tell the group how to prepare for the next lesson.

Each member should prepare for a meeting by writing answers for all of the background and discussion questions to be covered. If the group decides not to take an hour per week for private preparation, then expect to take at least two meetings per lesson to work through the questions. Application will be very difficult, however, without private thought and prayer.

Two reasons for studying in a group are accountability and support. When each member commits in front of the rest to seek growth in an area of life, you can pray with one another, listen jointly for God's guidance, help one another to resist temptation, assure each other that the other's growth matters to you, use the group to practice spiritual principles, and so on. Pray about one another's commitments and needs at most meetings. Spend the first few minutes of each meeting sharing any results from applications prompted by previous lessons. Then discuss new applications toward the end of the meeting. Follow such sharing with prayer for these and other needs.

If you write down each other's applications and prayer requests, you are more likely to remember to pray for them during the week, ask about them at the next meeting, and notice answered prayers. You might want to get a notebook for prayer requests and discussion notes.

Notes taken during discussion will help you to remember, follow up on ideas, stay on the subject, and clarify a total view of an issue. But don't let note-taking keep you from participating. Some groups choose one member at each meeting to take notes. Then someone copies the notes and distributes them at the next meeting. Rotating these tasks can help include people. Some groups have someone take notes on a large pad of paper or erasable marker board so that everyone can see what has been recorded.

Pages 114–115 lists some good sources of counsel for leading group studies.

PAUL AND PHILIPPI

Historical Background

Map of the Roman Empire

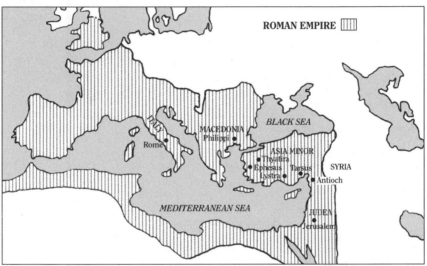

Paul wrote this note to his friends in Philippi as he sat in a Roman prison, yet the word *joy* is one of the most frequently used words in the letter. The reason for Paul's overflowing joy is found in some even more frequent words: *God, Lord, Christ,* and *Jesus.* It is a warm letter of thanks for kindness rendered, yet it contains some of the New Testament's deepest teaching about Christ and the gospel.

Saul the Pharisee

The man we call the apostle Paul was born in the first decade AD in Tarsus, a small but prosperous city on the trade route from Syria to Asia Minor. Tarsus was known for its schools of philosophy and liberal arts, and some scholars believe that Paul must have had some contact with these. Like most cities in the Roman Empire, Tarsus probably contained synagogues of Greek speaking Jews who were often as devout as their Hebrew-speaking brethren.[1]

Timeline of Paul's Ministry

(All dates are approximate, based on F. F. Bruce, *Paul: Apostle of the Heart Set Free*.)

Public ministry of Jesus	AD 28–30
Conversion of Paul (Acts 9:1-19)	33
Paul visits Jerusalem to see Peter (Galatians 1:18)	35
Paul in Cilicia and Syria (Galatians 1:21; Acts 9:30)	35–46
Paul visits Jerusalem to clarify the mission to the Gentiles (Galatians 2:1-10)	46
Paul and Barnabas in Cyprus and Galatia (Acts 13–14)	47–48
Letter to the Galatians	48?
Council of Jerusalem (Acts 15)	49
Paul and Silas travel from Antioch to Asia Minor, Macedonia, and Achaia (Acts 16–17)	49–50
Letters to the Thessalonians	50
Paul in Corinth (Acts 18:1-18)	50–52
Paul visits Jerusalem	52
Paul in Ephesus (Acts 19)	52–55
Letters to the Corinthians	55–56
Paul travels to Macedonia, Dalmatia, and Achaia (Acts 20)	55–57
Letter to the Romans	early 57
Paul to Jerusalem (Acts 21:1–23:22)	May 57
Paul imprisoned in Caesarea (Acts 23:23–26:32)	57–59
Paul sent to house arrest in Rome (Acts 27:1–28:31)	59–62
Letters to Philippians, Colossians, Ephesians, and Philemon	60?–62
Letters to Timothy and Titus	?
Paul executed in Rome	65?

However, in Philippians 3:5 Paul calls himself "a Hebrew of Hebrews," which probably means that his parents spoke Hebrew and raised him in a strict Jewish home, isolated as much as possible from the pagan city around them.[2] They named their boy "Saul" after Israel's first king, the most glorious member of the Israelite tribe of Benjamin, to which Saul's parents traced their ancestry (see Philippians 3:5). It was a rare Jew outside Palestine who could trace a pure lineage back to the ancient days of Israel, and fellow Jews would have envied the pedigree. Furthermore, Saul's family must have owned property and had some importance in the Gentile community as well, for Saul was born not only a citizen of Tarsus (see Acts 21:39) but also a citizen of Rome (see Acts 22:27-28).[3]

Saul was sent to study Jewish law in Jerusalem under the foremost rabbi of his day, the Pharisee Gamaliel (see Acts 22:3; Galatians 1:14). The Pharisees (the Hebrew word means "the separated ones") felt that God had set them apart to live by the *Torah* (the Law, or Teaching, of Moses). For them, this meant following the interpretations of the *Torah* laid down by generations of teachers. Some Pharisees held that a man was righteous if he had done more good than bad, but Saul apparently followed the stricter group who insisted that even the least implications of the Law must be kept.[4]

The Pharisees expected a *Messiah* (Hebrew for "Anointed One"; Greek: *Christ*), who would deliver them from foreign oppression and rule with justice. However, Jesus of Nazareth had infuriated many Pharisees by interpreting the Law differently and claiming a special relationship with God. Thus, when some Jews began to proclaim Jesus as Messiah and Lord (a term usually reserved for God), strict Pharisees opposed them vehemently.

Saul helped to lead the fight against the proclaimers of Christ in Jerusalem (see Acts 7:58-8:3; Galatians 1:13). When some were driven out, Saul obtained permission to pursue them to Damascus. But on the way there, Jesus confronted Saul in a blinding encounter (see Acts 9:1-19), revealing to Saul that he was persecuting the very God he professed to worship. From then on, Saul's understanding of God and the *Torah* began to change dramatically. He joined those Jews who were urging other Jews to believe in Jesus, and after some years God called him to proclaim Jesus as Savior to the Gentiles also. Saul took the Greek name "Paul" when he turned to work among Gentiles.

Paul the missionary

Paul's conversion may have marked his first move outward from cloistered Judaism into pagan culture. He spent ten years in the Roman provinces of Cilicia and Syria (see Galatians 1:21), probably preaching Jesus along with Hellenistic (Greek-speaking) Jewish Christians who had fled Jerusalem during the persecution. Then a believer named Barnabas called Paul from Tarsus to Syrian Antioch, where by this time rapid conversions had made the church more Gentile than Jewish.[5]

After a while, the church in Antioch commissioned Paul and Barnabas to evangelize the provinces of Cyprus and Galatia. The two men succeeded in founding churches in several cities. Indeed, the mission to the Gentiles was so successful that the apostles in Jerusalem invited Paul and Barnabas to a council to clarify exactly what God expected of Gentile believers (see Acts 15). Paul asserted that both Gentiles and Jews were reconciled to God by faith in Jesus, apart from keeping the Law, but certain Jewish Christians felt that Gentile converts must keep all the Jewish laws. The council confirmed Paul's view of the gospel, although some people thought that rejecting the laws as necessary to salvation would alienate potential Jewish converts. Those opponents remained Paul's enemies and continued to preach against him.

To Philippi

After the council in Jerusalem, Paul left Antioch with a new partner, Silas, to revisit the churches Paul had founded in Galatia. In a town called Lystra, they invited a young half-Jewish man—Timothy—to join their mission team. Along with his mother and grandmother, Timothy had accepted Christ during Paul's first visit to Lystra, and local church leaders now considered him an extremely promising disciple (see Acts 16:1-3; 2 Timothy 1:5).

Paul wanted to spend more time in Asia Minor (see the map of the Roman Empire on page 9), but the Holy Spirit seemed to be guiding them away from further evangelism there. Then Paul had a vision of a man urging him to "come over to Macedonia and help us" (see Acts 16:9). So, the team set out for the province of Macedonia, north of Greece. The first city they visited was Philippi, a Roman colony planted to guard the Roman road across Macedonia.

Because it was primarily a military outpost, Philippi contained too few Jews even to have a synagogue, which required ten adult men. Furthermore, Romans were notoriously anti-Semitic—about the time Paul arrived in Philippi, the Emperor declared Judaism a superstition and expelled all Jews from Rome.[6] So, the few Jews and sympathizers met at a "place of prayer" outside the gate of Philippi (see Acts 16:13); they were probably banned from meeting within the city limits.

The Jewish women and Gentile "God-fearers"[7] at the prayer place received the gospel warmly. Among them was Lydia, an independent businesswoman from Thyatira in Asia. Lydia invited the mission team to stay in her house, and for some weeks the converts continued to meet the missionaries at the prayer place. However, the team ran into trouble with the Roman authorities when Paul delivered a slave girl from demonic oppression. Her owners, who had been profiting from her ability to prophesy, accused Paul and Silas of disturbing the peace and trying to convert Romans. The city officials had Paul and Silas beaten and imprisoned.

That night, an earthquake shook the prison and freed all its prisoners. The jailer accepted Christ because of this miracle, and Paul and Silas agreed to remain in the prison. The next morning, the city magistrates ordered their release, but to protect themselves and future missionaries from similar mistreatment, Paul and Silas informed the officials that they had been treating Roman citizens like ordinary subjects, and demanded that the officials escort them out of town to uphold their honor.

So, Paul's mission team was scarcely in Philippi for a few weeks or months when they had to leave the fledgling church. The new believers had to live in a city where some people had been hurt economically by the missionaries, the magistrates had been embarrassed, and almost everyone was prejudiced against a supposed Jewish cult. Subtle discrimination and outright persecution were inevitable, yet the church flourished.

Partners

The Philippian Christians remained Paul's most loyal supporters. They sent him money when he was in Thessalonica, so that he would not have to live off the church he was founding there (see Philippians 4:16). Later, when they heard he was low on funds in Corinth, the Philippians sent money again (see 2 Corinthians 11:9). After that, they may have lost track of the apostle for years, until they heard that he was imprisoned, probably in Rome. It was ten years since Paul's first visit to Philippi. He was under arrest in a private house, so he had to pay rent and buy food, but the Christians in Rome would not support a missionary accused of an imperial crime. It was not illegal to be a Christian, so prudent people would have kept at arms' length someone Rome suspected of agitation and treason.

When they heard this news, the Philippians sent one of their members, Epaphroditus, to bear a gift of money to Paul and to take care of him while he was under arrest. But Epaphroditus became severely ill, and so Paul felt he should send the man back to Philippi to finish recovering. He sent Epaphroditus with a letter explaining the unexpected return, thanking the Philippians for their gift, informing them about his circumstances, and exhorting them to respond to their current situation as Christians should.

1. A. T. Robertson, "Paul, the Apostle," *The International Standard Bible Encyclopaedia*, vol. 4 (Grand Rapids, MI: Eerdmans, 1956), 2276.
2. F. F. Bruce, *Paul: Apostle of the Heart Set Free* (Grand Rapids, MI: Eerdmans, 1977), 41–43.
3. Bruce, 32–40.
4. Bruce, 50–52.
5. Bruce, 127–133.
6. Ralph P. Martin, *Philippians* (Grand Rapids, MI: Eerdmans, 1976), 5–6.
7. Acts 16:14 calls Lydia "a worshiper of God"; the Greek word means literally "God-fearer." Jews used this term to describe Gentiles who believed in the true God and joined in Jewish worship but did not fully convert and keep the Jewish laws. Because the meeting place is called a "prayer place" not a "synagogue," we infer that there were fewer than ten Jewish men but an unknown number of Jewish women and God-fearers. Jewish law required ten men for a "synagogue" but had no rules for a "prayer place."

OVERVIEW

This overview will probably take you more time than any other lesson of the study. If necessary, allow one week to read the "How to Use This Study" section on pages 5–8, the historical background on pages 9–13, and the whole letter to the Philippians. Then take a second week to answer the overview questions.

First impressions

The Philippians had not seen Paul for years. Then they heard he was under house arrest, and poorly supplied with food and other necessities. So, they sent Epaphroditus to take Paul some money and care for him during his ordeal. But now Epaphroditus is back unexpectedly. Surprised to see their emissary, but glad for news after months without word, the Philippians (if they treated letters as most people do) probably read through Paul's epistle quickly at first, searching for the main points and their friend's state of mind. They probably went back to study the profound words in detail later, but their first reading was likely to have been swift and general.

   In the same way, read through the whole of Paul's letter at one sitting. Get a general impression of his themes and state of mind.

Optional Application: Compare Paul's mood and the ideas he emphasizes to your own mood and the issues that preoccupy you. Is there anything in Paul's example that you would like to follow? Talk to God about this, and ask Him to renew your thinking (see Romans 12:2).

For Thought and Discussion: What clues does the letter give regarding Paul's circumstances? The situation in Philippi? The occasion that prompted the letter?

1. How would you describe the *mood* (emotion, state of mind) Paul conveys in this letter? What appear to be his attitudes toward his circumstances, the Philippians, other people, himself?

_____

_____

_____

_____

_____

_____

2. Repetition is a clue to the ideas that are most important in a book. What words and ideas are repeated in each of the following sets of verses?

1:27; 2:2-4; 4:2-3 _____

_____

1:5,7; 2:25; 4:14-15 _____

_____

1:4,18,25; 2:2,17-18; 3:1; 4:4,10 _____

_____

other _____

_____

Broad outline

If your impression of Philippians is vague after one reading, a broad outline can help sharpen it.

3. Reread Philippians, preferably in a different translation. (A different version can help you notice new things and can make a confusing passage clearer.)

This time, think of a short phrase or sentence that can serve as a title for each paragraph. You may want to include key words from the paragraph. Write your titles on the next page.

(Be creative. There is no one right answer; the first title is given as an example. Your Bible's paragraph divisions may differ, so feel free to alter those given here.)

1:1-2 _Servants to Saints_ _____

1:3-11 _____

_____

1:12-26 _____

_____

1:27-30 _____

_____

2:1-11 _____

_____

2:12-18 _____

_____

2:19-30 _____

_____

3:1-11 _____

_____

_____

3:12–4:1 _____

_____

_____

4:2-9 _____

_____

4:10-20 _____

_____

4:21-23 _____

_____

For Thought and Discussion: What title would you give to this letter?

Theme/purpose

People usually write letters in response to a particular situation in their own or their readers' lives. They normally have reasons for choosing the topics they cover in their letters. It is often not possible to reconstruct exactly what circumstances moved a person to write, but the more we can reconstruct, the better we will understand the writer's message.

Our own purpose for studying the letter will often differ from its original purpose, but how we understand and apply a writer's words should be influenced by how the Holy Spirit meant them to be understood and applied in the first century.

4. From your first readings of Philippians, what seem to be Paul's chief aims in writing this letter?

_____

_____

_____

_____

_____

_____

5. If you have not already done so, read the historical background on pages 9–13. If you feel that additional background would help you to better interpret Paul's letter, you might write down your questions here. Some of your questions may be answered later in this study guide. The sources in Study Aids on pages 111–115 may help you to answer others.

_____

_____

_____

_____

_____

6. In your first readings of Philippians, you may have come across questions you'd like answered as you go deeper into this study. While your thoughts are still fresh, you may want to jot down your questions here to serve as personal objectives for your investigation of the letter.

_____

_____

_____

_____

_____

Optional Application:
  a. If you were in prison, what kind of letter would you write to your friends? What would you talk about? How would your topics and feelings be like and unlike those Paul expresses?
  b. Ask God to give you Paul's attitudes toward prison, life, enemies, and so on. Be specific about how you want to change.

Study Skill — Application

James 1:22 urges us to do what the Word says, not merely listen to it. So, the last step of Bible study is asking yourself, "What difference should this passage make in my life? How should it make me want to think or act?" Application will require time, thought, prayer, and perhaps even discussion with another person.

At times, you may find it most productive to concentrate on one specific application, giving it careful thought and prayer. At other times, you may want to list many implications a passage of Scripture has for your life, and then choose one to concentrate on for prayer and action. Use whatever method helps you grow more obedient to God's Word.

---

7. You have been reading Philippians as just an ordinary ancient letter, but it is also God's Word to us today. Does your first reading of Philippians suggest any areas in which it might apply to you? If so, what are some of those areas?

_____

_____

_____

_____

_____

_____

_____

For the group

This "For the group" section and the ones in later lessons are intended to suggest ways of structuring your discussions. Feel free to select and adapt what suits your group. The main goals of this lesson are to get to know the book of Philippians as a whole and the people with whom you are going to study it.

Worship. Some groups like to begin with prayer and/or singing. Some share requests for prayer at the beginning, but leave the actual prayer until after the study. Others prefer just to chat and have refreshments for a while and then move to the study, leaving worship until the end.

Warm-up. The beginning of a new study is a good time to lay a foundation for honest sharing of ideas, to get comfortable with each other, and to encourage a sense of common purpose. One way to establish common ground is to talk about what each group member hopes to get out of your group — out of your study of Philippians, and out of any prayer, singing, sharing, outreach, or anything else you might do together. Why do you want to study the Bible? If you have someone write down each member's hopes and expectations, then you can look back at these goals later to see if they are being met. Allow about fifteen minutes for this discussion.

How to use this study. If the group has never used a LIFECHANGE study guide before, you might take a whole meeting to get acquainted, discuss your goals for the study, and go over the "How to Use This Study" section on pages 5–8. Then you can take a second meeting to discuss the historical background on pages 9–13 and the overview questions. This will give you more time to read Philippians and prepare lesson 1 for discussion.

It is a good idea to clear up any confusion about how to do the study as soon as possible, so at the beginning of your second meeting, ask the group if anyone was confused about how to do lesson 1.

Reading. It is often helpful to refresh everyone's memory by reading the passage aloud before beginning to discuss your lesson. Reading the whole letter may take time, but the effort will be rewarded. Have a different person read each chapter, using the tone of voice he or she thinks Paul was trying to convey so that the letter sounds like the work of a living person. It should take perhaps fifteen minutes to read all of Philippians.

First impressions. Ask the group to share first impressions of Philippians — its style, mood, content, or whatever strikes the group. If members don't understand the question, you might ask them how Paul's letter is like and unlike letters they write or receive, or like and unlike a sermon, a graduation speech, or advice from a father. The point of question 1 is to help the group see Philippians as a real letter from a person to real people for a specific occasion. Don't spend more than a few minutes on this question.

The setting of a letter is an important part of its context. The background on pages 9–13 may help you to understand the setting. Ask several group members to tell who Paul was, how he got to know the Philippians, what is important to know about the Philippians, and what was going on in Paul's and the Philippians' lives when Paul wrote. By piecing together everyone's recollections of the background, you can probably recall the main points. Then, using the background and clues from the letter, see how much you can conclude about why Paul was writing and what was going on at the time.

To help the group get to know Paul as a real person, ask them to share what kind of person they think he was (based on the background and the letter). Application will require you to put yourselves in Paul's shoes, and it will be easier to identify with Paul if he seems real to you.

Looking for repeated words and ideas (question 2) should help the group see themes and main ideas in the letter. You might ask the group to name as many repeated phrases and ideas as possible, and then move to question 4 on the letter's themes. You could share your titles (question 3) after that. Remember that there is no one right way to title a passage.

21

Questions. Give everyone a chance to share questions about the letter or the way you are studying it. It is good to clear up confusion about the book, the group, or the study guide as early as possible. You may want to leave some questions about the book until later in your study; they may answer themselves as you go deeper if you are looking for the answers. You could point out the list of references on pages 111–115 or encourage members to seek answers from their pastors or other Christians they respect.

Application. Question 7 ties in with the expectations and objectives you discussed at the beginning of your meeting. If some group members are unfamiliar with how to apply God's Word to their lives in specific ways, this is a chance to think of some sample applications together. (You could do this next week if you are running out of time.) Application is often the most difficult part of the study, since many people have never been taught how to apply Scripture consciously, yet it is essential to the Christian life.

Wrap up. The group leader should have read through lesson 2 and its "For the group" section. At this point, he or she might give a short summary of what members can expect in that lesson and in the coming meeting. This is a chance to whet everyone's appetite, assign any optional questions, omit any numbered questions, or forewarn members of any possible difficulties.

You might also encourage any members who found the overview especially hard. Some people are better at seeing the big picture or the whole of a book than others. Some are best at analyzing a particular verse or paragraph, while others are strongest at seeing how a passage applies to our lives. Urge members to give thanks for their own and others' strengths, and to give and request help when needed. The group is a place to learn from each other. Later lessons will draw on the gifts of close analyzers as well as overviewers and appliers, practical as well as theoretical thinkers.

Worship. Many groups like to end with singing and/or prayer. This can include songs and prayers that respond to what you've learned in Philippians or prayers for specific needs of group members. Many people are shy about sharing personal needs or praying aloud in groups, especially before they know the other people well. If this is true of your group, then a song and/or some silent prayer, and a short closing prayer spoken by the leader, might be an appropriate end. You could share requests and pray in pairs instead, if appropriate.

PHILIPPIANS 1:1-11

A Prayer for Partners

Paul begins his letter with the form customary in his time. He identifies first the senders and then the receivers (see 1:1). He writes a greeting next (see 1:2), and follows with a prayer for the readers' continuing blessing (see 1:3-11). However, for Paul, the form is not mere empty convention; he uses it to glorify Christ and upbuild the Philippians.

Read 1:1-11 slowly. A second reading in another translation would be helpful. Look for repetition and for Paul's overall train of thought.

Servants to saints (1:1-2)

Servants (1:1). "Bond-servants" in NASB. The word means slaves who belong to a master. The Old Testament describes holy men as "servants of God," but Paul puts Jesus on the Father's level.

God's holy people (1:1). Literally, "holy ones" or "set apart ones." In keeping with the theme of this letter, Paul writes to *all* the holy people, not just the leaders. (Note the word *all* in 1:4.)

Overseers (1:1). In the second century AD, this word "bishops" (KJV) came to mean the chief elder or pastor in a city, but in Paul's time there were apparently several "overseers" in the Philippian church.

Deacons (1:1). Literally, "servants," a more general term than "slaves." Acts 6:1-7 tells the origin of

For Thought and Discussion: What do Paul and the Philippians have in common that makes them partners (see 1:6-7; 2:1-2)?

this office among Christians: deacons were servants/ministers to the sick, poor, hungry, and those with spiritual wounds.

Grace (1:2). The normal Greek greeting was *cherein*, meaning "greetings" or "favor from me to you." Paul preferred a related word, *charis*, which named God's favor bestowed on sinful man with no strings attached. This greeting reminded the Philippians of God's gift of redemption through His Son's death, and wished them continuing favor from God to face daily needs.[1]

Peace (1:2). This was the normal Jewish greeting. It meant wholeness and well-being in all aspects of life—health, harmony between people, a flourishing earth, and so on. To wish someone peace was to wish him a foretaste of the Messianic Age foretold by the prophets, a taste of God's presence and the fulfillment that flows from that presence.[2]

Thanks and prayer (1:3-11)

Partnership (1:5). "A joint participation in a common interest or activity."[3] "Fellowship" (KJV) or "participation" (NASB). *Koinonia* was also the Greek word for a business partnership or a community.[4]

1. Paul thanks God with joy for the Philippians because they are his partners in the gospel (see 1:3-5). Observe how they are his partners.

   a. What are the goals of this partnership (see 1:7,12,27)?

   _____

   _____

   _____

   _____

   _____

b. How have the Philippians shown their participation with Paul (see 1:19; 2:25; 4:14-18)?

_____

_____

_____

_____

_____

Optional Application: How often do you remember other Christians and thank God for them? Try doing this.

c. In what other way can they demonstrate their partnership (see 1:27-30)?

_____

_____

_____

_____

d. How does Paul show his partnership with the Philippians (see 1:3-4,7-11,23-26)?

_____

_____

_____

_____

2. How could you act as a partner with other Christians in God's service?

_____

_____

_____

_____

_____

Optional
Application: How
should Paul's confi-
dence in 1:6 lead you
to regard your own
future and "good
work"? Try meditating
on verse 6.

For Thought and
Discussion: What dif-
ference would it make
to a person's life if
he or she knew that
God will complete the
work He starts in any
believer?

Optional
Application: List
some practical ways
in which a person can
love others with the
"affection of Christ
Jesus" (1:8). Choose
one to act upon.

> **Study Skill — Cross References**
> Other parts of Scripture can often shed light on
> the passage you are studying. These other pas-
> sages are called *cross references*.

3. The Philippians have behaved as partners with
   Paul "from the first day [that we met] until
   now" (1:5), and Paul is confident of something
   for the future (see 1:6).

   a. What "good work" did God begin in the
      Philippians (see Philippians 1:6; Romans
      8:28-29)?

      _____

      _____

      _____

   b. What does Paul mean when he says that God
      will carry this work "on to completion until
      the day of Christ Jesus" (Philippians 1:6)?

      _____

      _____

      _____

   c. Why can Paul be perfectly certain that the
      "good work" will be completed? (What is the
      basis of his confidence?)

      _____

      _____

      _____

      _____

4. Gratitude for the Philippians' partnership leads
   Paul to the prayer of 1:9-11. What does he ask
   God for?

   (see verse 9) _____

   _____

so that (see verse 10) _____

_____

and so that (see verse 10) _____

_____

and so that (see verse 11) _____

_____

for the ultimate goal of (see verse 11) _____

_____

_____

5. From 1:9, why is it important that our love abound in . . .

"knowledge" (of God, of His truth)?

_____

_____

_____

"depth of insight" (moral judgment, discernment of best methods)?

_____

_____

_____

_____

For Thought and Discussion: How is it possible for your love to grow? What does God need to do? What do you need to do?

Optional Application: How can you pursue greater knowledge of God, insight, or the ability to discern true from false and good from bad?

For Further Study: On question 5, see 1 John 4:7-8.

For Thought and Discussion: Does God expect us to be flawless? What does He expect (see Philippians 1:10; 2 Corinthians 4:7)?

Pure (1:10). Literally, "sincere" in NASB and KJV. Fine pottery was fragile in ancient times, and it often cracked when fired. Instead of discarding flawed pottery, dishonest merchants often filled in the cracks with a hard wax. The wax was undetectable in a shop but could be seen when held up to sunlight. Honest merchants marked their unflawed pottery *sine cera* ("without wax") because it held up to sun-testing.[5]

Optional Application: Write out a prayer for someone that expresses the spirit of Paul's prayer in 1:9-11. (What feelings and desires does Paul express?)

For Further Study: How is it possible to bear the "fruit of righteousness" (see Philippians 1:11; John 15:1-5)?

Optional Application.
a. What can we learn from 1:3-11 about how to pray for each other?
b. Commit yourself to pray for a few other people according to Paul's example.

Blameless (1:10). Literally, "not stumbled against," that is, not a stumbling block to others.[6]

6. Why are purity and blamelessness crucial Christian traits (see 1:10; 2:15-16)?

_____

_____

_____

_____

_____

7. What sorts of fruits result from being rightly related to God (see 1:11)? (*Optional*: See Matthew 5:1-10,38-48; 25:37-40; Galatians 5:22-23.)

_____

_____

_____

_____

Study Skill — Summarizing
Summarizing a passage after you have studied it verse by verse can often help you to remember what the whole is about. You can refine your title for the passage or summarize it in a sentence.

---

8. Look back at the title you gave to 1:3-11 on page 17. Then, try to summarize this passage in a sentence.

_____

_____

_____

_____

9. a. What is the most significant insight you have had from your study of 1:1-11?

_____

_____

_____

_____

b. Does this insight suggest any area of your life in which you could respond to Paul's words? If so, what further prayer or action seems appropriate, if any?

_____

_____

_____

_____

_____

10. If you have any questions about anything covered in this study, write them here. Plan to seek answers from your study group, from written sources such as those listed in Study Aids on pages 111–115, or from some person you trust.

_____

_____

_____

_____

For Thought and Discussion: a. What encourages this sense of partnership among Christians? Name some of the attitudes, circumstances, or practices you think are necessary.

b. How could you encourage attitudes between yourself and other Christians like those between Paul and the Philippians?

For Thought and Discussion: What do you learn about God's and Jesus' nature from 1:1-11?

For Thought and Discussion: Think about 1:10. How do you think it would affect a person's life if every day he or she thought about Christ's imminent return?

For the group

Worship.

Warm-up. Some groups like to begin each meeting with a brief warm-up or ice-breaker question to get members' minds focused on the topic at hand. For this meeting, you could try something like, "What does the word *fellowship* mean to you? Give an example of Christian fellowship." The question is meant to draw out people's preconceptions, so that Paul's use of the word *fellowship* or *partnership* can be contrasted with popular understandings of the word. Don't let anyone jump into Philippians just yet.

Read aloud. Ask someone to read 1:1-11 aloud to refresh everyone's memory.

Summary. It's easy, and frustrating, to get so lost in the details of verse-by-verse study that you forget what Paul is talking about. To help avoid this, have someone quickly summarize what is said in 1:1-11. You can let two or three people summarize at this point, but don't be concerned if they are vague or see the passage differently. If you return to a summary at the end of your discussion, you will probably find the group much more articulate.

Background. Treat the word definitions and other text in the study guide as background. Urge group members to ignore whatever they cannot absorb; they can return to it when they study Philippians again in the future. Try not to get sidetracked discussing individual words.

Questions. The questions cover essentially these topics:

> Partnership (questions 1–2)
> God's good work (question 3)
> Paul's prayer (questions 4–7)
> Summary (question 8)
> Application (question 9)

If the group has prepared well, you should be able to spend about half your time discussing what the passage means, and about half discussing how it applies to each of you. You may prefer to discuss applications of each topic as you come to them, or to interpret the whole passage and then go back and apply it. For instance,

> question 1 — Observe and interpret about partnership.
> question 2 — Apply the idea of partnership to your lives.
> question 3 — Observe and interpret about God's good work.

What are the implications of God's work for you?
questions 4–7 — Observe and interpret about what Paul prays for.
How can you apply these observations about Paul's prayer?

Feel free to focus on one or two of these topics, to cover some of the optional questions, and/or to omit some of the numbered questions in your discussion.

Summary. Ask one or two people to summarize the main points of your discussion and Paul's words in 1:1-11.

Worship. When you close in prayer, ask God to shape your group into partners as Paul and the Philippians were. Ask Him to show you how to be partners with other Christians. You might pray 1:9-11 for each other also.

Practicing Partnership. Your group is an ideal place in which to begin practicing the kind of partnership Paul talks about. How could you begin to think and act more like partners? You could pray daily for each other along the lines of 1:9-11. You could look for ways to encourage each other in love, knowledge, and insight. You could express appreciation for each other as Paul does. What other ways can you think of?

1. James Montgomery Boice, *Philippians: An Expositional Commentary* (Grand Rapids, MI: Zondervan, 1971), 27–30.
2. Hartmut Beck and Colin Brown, "Peace," *The New International Dictionary of New Testament Theology*, vol. 2, (Grand Rapids, MI: Zondervan, 1986), 776–783.
3. Kenneth Wuest, *Philippians in the Greek New Testament* (Grand Rapids, MI: Eerdmans, 1942), 31.
4. Jerry Bridges, *True Fellowship* (Colorado Springs, CO: NavPress, 1985), 17. See also William Hendriksen, *Exposition of Philippians* (Grand Rapids, MI: Baker, 1962), 93.
5. Boice, 55.
6. Wuest, 37.

Lesson Three
PHILIPPIANS 1:12-26
The Important Thing

The Philippians had sent Epaphroditus to Paul because they had heard that Paul was in need. Since Epaphroditus' departure, they had probably heard nothing of Paul. They may well have supposed that his ministry was at a standstill and that he was understandably depressed. But the news Epaphroditus brought was different.

Read 1:12-26 with the eagerness the Philippians might have felt for news from Paul. Think about how remarkable Paul's attitudes are.

1. What is Paul talking about in this passage?

_____

_____

_____

_____

Optional Application: Has God "chained" you to anyone (in a hospital bed, office, and so on) in order to share the gospel (see 1:13)? If so, how can you use those chains to God's advantage?

Palace guard (1:13). The praetorian guard was a special class of Roman soldiers. If Paul was in Rome, then this was the emperor's official bodyguard, who also watched imperial prisoners.

Chains (1:13). This Greek word means a "short length of chain by which the wrist of a prisoner was bound to the wrist of the soldier who was his guard, so that escape was impossible."[1]

For Thought and Discussion: List all the character traits you can discover about Paul in 1:12-26.

Optional Application: How might your circumstances serve to advance the gospel?

For Thought and Discussion: Do you ever lose your courage in sharing the gospel (see 1:14)? If so, what kinds of situations discourage you? How would Paul overcome such discouragement?

While awaiting trial, Paul was allowed to rent private rooms, but he was chained 24 hours a day to a soldier. As each soldier took his turn chained to Paul, he was a captive audience hearing Paul pray, read Scripture, dictate letters, and receive visitors. Paul may have preached directly to the guards and taken a personal interest in them. A prisoner who cared about his guards and who had such strange beliefs as Paul had would have aroused interest among the soldiers. Paul spent two years under this house arrest in Rome (see Acts 28:16,20,30-31).

Everyone else (1:13). The pagans in charge of Paul's case certainly heard his beliefs and saw his character.

2. How does Paul feel about his circumstances (see 1:18)?

_____

_____

_____

3. He feels this way first of all because *his circumstances are serving to advance the gospel* (see 1:12-18). How has his imprisonment affected . . .

other Christians in Rome (see 1:14-18)?

_____

_____

_____

_____

the pagans in the palace guard, and others (see 1:13)?

_____

_____

_____

4. Why is Paul unconcerned about the selfishness of those who preach Christ in order to make trouble for Paul (see 1:17-18)?

_____

_____

_____

_____

For Further Study: Compare Philippians 1:15-18 to Galatians 1:6-9. In what case is Paul angry about people who preach for selfish motives? In what cases is he not angry?

Deliverance (1:19). Or, "salvation." That is, Paul's release from prison (see 1:25), his deliverance from affliction by death, or his spiritual salvation.[2]

Ashamed (1:20). Or, "disappointed."[3]

Optional Application: Are you in any situation with other preachers similar to the one Paul was in (see 1:17-18)? If so, how can you apply Paul's attitude to your situation?

5. Paul's second reason for joy is his certainty that his *circumstances will result in his deliverance* (see 1:19-20). Paul will regard either execution or release from prison as deliverance because he eagerly expects and hopes something (see 1:20).

a. How will Christ be exalted if Paul lives (see 1:20-26)?

_____

_____

_____

_____

_____

Optional Application: What hinders you from having Paul's attitudes toward people and circumstances? What can you do about these obstacles? Ask God to show you.

b. How will Christ be exalted if Paul dies?

_____

_____

_____

_____

Optional Application: Whom do you know who needs you for their "progress and joy in the faith" (1:25)? What can you do to meet this need? Talk to God about this.

Optional Application:
    a. Why does Paul regard death as gain?
    b. Write down two ways the statement "For to me, to live is Christ and to die is gain" (1:21) could affect your life.

For Thought and Discussion: What did you learn in 1:12-26 about God and Jesus?

c. Meditate on 1:20 and its implications for you. How can Christ be *exalted* in *your body* by your *life* or by your *death*?

_____

_____

_____

_____

_____

_____

_____

6. How does Paul show what he means by "to me, to live is Christ" (1:21)? (*Optional*: See 1:1,27; 2:5; 3:3,7-14; 4:13.)

_____

_____

_____

_____

_____

7. Look back at what you said 1:12-26 was about in question 1. Then, summarize Paul's attitudes in his situation.

_____

_____

_____

_____

_____

_____

Study Skill — Outlining

One way to show yourself the connections in a writer's train of thought is to outline what he says. You first summarize the main message of the work (the whole letter) in a phrase or sentence. Then you summarize each of its main sections (groups of paragraphs). Finally, you add supporting ideas (paragraphs, and then single verses). An outline of Philippians might begin like this:

[The overall purpose or message of Philippians]
   I. (1:1-2) Greetings: Servants to Saints
  II. [The main idea of 1:3-11]
     A. [a supporting point]
     B. [a supporting point]
 III. [The main idea of 1:12-26]
     [and so on]

For Further Study: Try outlining 1:1-26.

For Thought and Discussion: Count the number of times Paul speaks of *knowing* in chapter 1. Why does he emphasize knowledge rather than feelings? (Look for what he says about knowing and thinking in the rest of the letter.)

8. a. Which one of the attitudes Paul expresses in 1:12-26 seems especially relevant to your current circumstances?

_____

_____

_____

_____

_____

b. How could you follow Paul's example with regard to this attitude?

_____

_____

_____

_____

_____

> ## Study Skill — Application
>
> It may be easier to think of a specific application if you begin with a general one and gradually make it more specific. For instance, to say, "'To live is Christ', means that I should spend time in His presence and do what He wants me to do!" is a first step toward working out the implications of what Paul says. To say, "'To live is Christ' means I need to commit myself to a half hour of prayer daily and spend more time loving my coworkers and less time worrying about bills" is a next step. You can make "more time loving my coworkers" more specific by saying, "To accomplish this goal I need to meditate on Christ daily, repeat Philippians 1:21 to myself frequently during the day, and ask God to increase this attitude in me. I will have lunch with Barbara and find out what is going on in her life and how I can support her."

9. List any questions you have about 1:12-26.

_____

_____

_____

_____

_____

_____

For the group

Worship.

Read aloud.

Summarize.

Paul's circumstances advance the gospel. When you discuss this passage, you may want to quickly ask some of the observation questions that the study guide either answers or skips over. For instance, since Paul talks about his circumstances in this passage, have someone describe the circumstances he was in.

Discuss your personal responses to being chained to another person for two years. Consider privacy, freedom, fresh air, and so on. This will help the group identify with Paul and feel how uncommon his attitudes are. After covering question 2, ask, "What is one reason why Paul feels this way, according to verses 12-18?" Then cover questions 3 and 4.

At this point, you might discuss one of the Optional Applications on verses 12-18 (pages 35–37). Encourage each person to think about how he or she could have attitudes like Paul's and what difference these attitudes could make to the way he or she deals with life. It might be helpful to examine the obstacles that hinder you from being like Paul. What habits, assumptions, and so on get in your way? Try to apply Paul's attitudes to specific circumstances you are facing.

Paul's circumstances will result in his deliverance. You can handle Paul's second reason for joy similarly. First, what is his second reason? Next, what does Paul mean by this (questions 5 and 6)? Third, what do Paul's words mean for you?

The Optional Applications on page 38 offer some ways to explore applications, and most of the group will have thought of responses to question 8. You could give each person a chance to explain, "This week, for me to live is Christ means . . ." or, "Christ will be exalted in my body if (or because) I . . ." or, "For me, to die is gain, and therefore . . ."

Encourage the group to use the way Paul exalted Christ or lived a Christ-centered life as a model for their actions. Also, urge the group to think of specific responses. Not everyone will want to share his applications with the group. Try to discern how much encouragement is appropriate for each individual.

Prayer. Thank God for Paul's example, and for the Holy Spirit in you who prompts and enables you to follow Paul's example. Ask God to show you how your circumstances could advance the gospel, how you could exalt Christ in your life, and how your death could be gain for you and glory for Christ.

Civic Pride in Philippi

The Romans were in the habit of settling retired army veterans in strategic parts of their Empire. The veterans were honored with the rights of Roman citizenship as well as with land to use and bequeath to heirs. The citizens of these colonies were always enormously proud of their identities as Romans, fully understood the value of their status, and so were utterly loyal. They modeled their city government after Rome's, including official titles (see Acts 16:20). The colony of Philippi possessed fertile soil, gold and silver mines, and a toll gate on the trade route between Asia and Europe. The Philippians could not have asked for a better situation, and they owed it to Rome.[4]

This background helps to explain Paul's instruction to "conduct yourselves in a manner worthy . . ." in 1:27 and his reference to "citizenship" in 3:20 (see pages 43–44 and 89). The Philippian Christians had been brought up to find their identity and pride in Roman citizenship, to make Rome and Philippi their first loyalty. Paul wanted them to identify first of all with a different city and kingdom.

---

1. William Barclay, *The Letters to the Philippians, Colossians, and Thessalonians* (Philadelphia: Westminster, 1975), 22.
2. Kenneth Barker, ed., *The NIV Study Bible* (Grand Rapids, MI: Zondervan, 1985), 1804.
3. James Montgomery Boice, *Philippians: An Expositional Commentary* (Grand Rapids, MI: Zondervan, 1971), 73; C. G. Moule, *The Epistle to the Philippians* (Grand Rapids, MI: Baker, 1981), 23.
4. Ralph P. Martin, *Philippians* (Grand Rapids, MI: Eerdmans, 1976), 2–9; J. Sidlow Baxter, *Explore the Book*, vol. 6 (Grand Rapids, MI: Zondervan, 1960), 181–183.

PHILIPPIANS 1:27-2:4

Worthy Conduct

In 1:12-26, Paul has been speaking of his own attitudes toward his painful circumstances. Now, in 1:27 he turns to the Philippians' responses to their circumstances. He has told how he views pagans and Christians in Rome (see 1:12-18); now he describes how his readers should view pagans and Christians in Philippi. He has given thanks for his partnership with the Philippians (see 1:3-8), but now he speaks of their partnership with each other.

Read 1:27–2:18 to follow the whole of Paul's train of thought on this subject. This passage contains one of the finest hymns in Scripture and a foundational statement of the doctrine of Christ, yet Paul states it not to teach something new but to motivate the Philippians to action. Notice how Paul expects doctrine to affect life.

Opposition (1:27-30)

Manner (1:27). "Conversation" in KJV. The Greek word is *polteuo*, from which we get "polite" and "political." A *polis* was the basic unit of Greek society—an independent city-state. In imperial times, citizens of a Roman colony like Philippi regarded the whole Empire as their *polis* in one sense, and their city as their *polis* in another. They took their privileges and duties as citizens of Rome and Philippi extremely seriously, with great patriotism and pride.

For Thought and Discussion: How do people suffer for Christ today (see 1:29)?

For Thought and Discussion: What is the "sign" in verse 28?

Optional Application:
a. Choose one of the reasons Paul gives for promoting the gospel fearlessly, and think about it. Does it motivate you to contend for the gospel? Why or why not?
b. How could you contend along with other Christians for the faith?

Thus, when Paul says, "Only let your *politeuo* be worthy of the gospel," he means, "let your fulfillment of duties as citizens of God's Kingdom and members of Christ's partnership/community be worthy of that citizenship."[1] (See also the box, "Civic Pride in Philippi" on page 42, and the definition of "citizenship" on page 89.)

1. The Philippians were experiencing opposition from the pagans in their city (see 1:28). What kind of response to this opposition was worthy of their citizenship in Christ's kingdom (see 1:27-30)?

_____

_____

_____

_____

_____

_____

2. What reasons does Paul give for promoting the gospel fearlessly?

1:27 _____

_____

1:28 _____

_____

1:29 _____

_____

1:30 _____

_____

Imitating Christ (2:1-4)

3. In 2:1-2, Paul calls the Philippians to reflect on the blessings of their common life in Christ.

a. What are these four blessings (see 2:1)?

_____

_____

_____

_____

_____

b. In what four ways should we respond because of our common experience as Christians (see 2:2)?

_____

_____

_____

_____

_____

Optional Application: How could you increasingly adopt the attitude that suffering for Christ is a privilege that has been "granted to you" (1:29)? How does this attitude apply to your current circumstances?

For Thought and Discussion: Paul is describing group conduct in 1:27–2:18. How can you encourage the attitude of 1:27-28 in your church or fellowship group?

Study Skill — Connecting Words

Connecting words are clues to the logic in a passage. Connectives may show:

Time: *after, as, before, them, until, when, while*

Place: *where*

Reason: *because, for, since*

Purpose: *in order that, so that*

Contrast: *although, but, much more, nevertheless, otherwise, yet*

Comparison: *also, as, as . . . so, just as . . . so, likewise, so also*

Source: *by means of, from, through*

The NIV often supplies connecting words that are only implied in the original Greek (such as "Then" in 2:2). This is done to help the reader follow Paul's logic.

For Thought and Discussion: What is the difference between unity and uniformity? What would happen if all Christians had the same opinions and tastes?

4. Summarize 2:1-4.

If (see verse 1) _____

_____

_____

_____

then (see verses 2-4) _____

_____

_____

_____

_____

_____

Common sharing in the Spirit (2:1). *Koinonia*, the same word as "partnership" in 1:5 (RSV: "participation"). Paul could mean the communion between us and the Spirit, or the communion we have with each other because we each share in God's Spirit.

Compassion (2:1). "Mercies" in KJV; "affection" in RSV and NASB. God's emotions of care (see James 5:11; Romans 12:1; 2 Corinthians 1:3).[2]

5. How have you experienced one of the blessings in 2:1? (For instance, what encouragement from Christ have you received? Or, how has God's love comforted you?)

_____

_____

_____

_____

_____

_____

Like-minded (2:2). Having the same attitudes, not necessarily the same opinions.[3] "Not uniformity in thought but the common disposition to work together and serve one another—the 'attitude' of Christ (see 2:5)."[4]

For Thought and Discussion: Is it wrong ever to think of your own interests (see 2:4)? Why or why not?

6. According to verses 2:3-4, what attitudes are the opposite of "selfish ambition" and "vain conceit"?

   a. _____

   _____

   _____

   b. _____

   _____

Optional Application: How can you practice 2:1-4 toward other members of your church or fellowship group?

7. a. In your own words, describe one of the desirable attitudes in 2:2-4 that does not come naturally to you.

   _____

   _____

   _____

   _____

   b. Why should any of the blessings Paul names in 2:1 motivate you to have the attitude you just described?

   _____

   _____

   _____

   _____

   _____

   _____

For Thought and Discussion:
a. From 2:1-8, does it seem that humility means feeling worthless or inferior? What was Jesus' model?
b. Why is it difficult for most of us to consider others better than ourselves?

For Further Study: What does humility (see 2:3) mean? Look at Jesus' teaching in Luke 6:41-43; 18:9-14; 22:24-27; John 13:3-5,12-17.

Optional Application: One step to humility is to focus your mind on other people's needs and worth (see Philippians 2:3-4). Another step is to focus on God's purposes and worth (see 1 Peter 5:6). Try turning your thoughts to God and others for a day. Each time you catch yourself thinking about self, confess and ask God for grace to attend to Him (see 2 Corinthians 10:4-5).

Study Skill — Application Notebook

A notebook can remind you of the instruction from God that you are meditating on, and it can help you to organize your thoughts and intentions. For example, perhaps you want to look not only to your own interests, but also to the interests of others. You could try one or two of the following approaches:

1. Memorize Philippians 2:4 or 2:1-4.

2. Ask God to enable you to notice others' interests and how to serve them. Confess that on your own you are really most concerned about your own wants.

3. Write down the names of two or three people, along with some of their interests/needs and how they might conflict with yours.

4. For the next week, be alert for times when you have to choose whether to look out for others' interests. As soon after each time as possible write down what the choice was and what you decided.

other's interest:	my interest:	decision:
Bill's need to be listened to and respected	protecting myself emotionally from rebuke	take Bill to lunch and decide to be excited about his visit

5. At the end of each day, review your list from (3) or (4). Confess to God the times when you chose not to serve another person's interest. Confess that you probably noticed only a few of the chances you had to serve. Ask for grace to make the right choices tomorrow. Relax in the knowledge that God will complete His good work in you (see 1:6).

---

8. a. What one truth from 1:27–2:4 would you like to apply in your own dealings with other Christians or non-Christians this week?

_____

_____

_____

_____

_____

_____

b. What concrete steps can you take to put this
teaching into practice?

_____

_____

_____

_____

_____

_____

9. List any questions you have about 1:27–2:4.

_____

_____

_____

_____

**For Thought and
Discussion:** What
did you learn about
God and Christ from
1:27–2:4?

For the group

Worship.

Read aloud. To put this week's passage in context,
have someone read all of 1:27–2:18 aloud. Explain
that the next lessons will cover 2:5-18.

Summarize. First summarize 1:27–2:18, then
1:27–2:4.

Opposition. Cover questions 1 and 2, then lead the
group to explore how 1:27-30 applies to you. The
Optional Applications suggest several ways of doing
this.
    Paul told the Philippians to contend *together*
for the faith (see 1:27). How can you do this as a
group? Begin with diligent prayer. Then if you can,
make a specific plan, and carry it out during the

next few weeks. For instance, you can pray together consistently for unbelievers you know, serve the needy in your community in Christ's name, hold a Bible study for non-Christians, or even get involved in some local social issue. If you can't think of any appropriate evangelism or outreach, talk to some local pastors about the needs they perceive.

Imitating Christ. Question 4 summarizes the paragraph. After that, go through each incentive in 2:1, asking group members to describe how they have experienced each (question 5). Then discuss the conduct that Paul says should flow from those experiences (questions 6 and 7). Finally, give each person a chance to share how he plans to respond to Paul's words. With so little to interpret, you should have plenty of time to discuss application.

Growing together. By your fourth meeting you may know each other well enough to share the weaknesses you perceive in yourselves. Partnership includes trusting each other and being worthy of that trust. Partnership also includes sharing responsibility to pray for and encourage each other. As you reveal desires, efforts, successes, and failures, you give one another chances to practice love, humility, and concern for others' interests. You can learn from each other how to act on God's grace to grow in character, and how to respond when you fail as you grow.

You might discuss ways of applying Paul's teaching in your group. For instance, how can you cultivate unity of spirit, purpose, love, and attitude? How could you contend as one person for the faith of the gospel?

Summarize your discussion, and settle any plans for your next meeting.

Prayer. Thank God for encouragement in Christ, comfort from His love, common sharing in the Spirit, His tenderness and compassion, and the privilege of suffering for and serving Him. Pray for one another to be able to fulfill your intentions for obedience.

1. Kenneth Wuest, *Philippians in the Greek New Testament* (Grand Rapids, MI: Eerdmans, 1942), 48; James Montgomery Boice, *Philippians: An Expositional Commentary* (Grand Rapids, MI: Zondervan, 1971), 101–103.
2. Boice, 117.
3. Ralph P. Martin, *Philippians* (Grand Rapids, MI: Eerdmans, 1976), 66, 88; C. G. Moule, *The Epistle to the Philippians*, (Grand Rapids, MI: Baker, 1981), 35.
4. Kenneth Barker, ed., *The NIV Study Bible* (Grand Rapids, MI: Zondervan, 1985), 1805.

PHILIPPIANS 2:5-11

The Mindset of Christ

Jesus was alive in Palestine only thirty years before Paul wrote to the Philippian church. Yet Paul stated 2:6-11 not as an amazing teaching of which he wanted to convince his readers, but as a body of agreed fact that should lead the Philippians to certain behavior.

Read 2:5-11 with a fresh sense of wonder at what God has done. Look at several translations if you have them.

1. What is the connection between 2:5-11 and 1:27–2:4?

_____

_____

_____

_____

_____

For Further Study:
How is it possible to have your mindset or mind (see 2:5) changed? See Romans 12:2; 8:3-13,26-30; Psalm 86:11; 119:11, 33-40.

Mindset (2:5). "Mind" in KJV and RSV. The Greek word *phroneite* and related words (*phronein*) mean mind, feeling, a mental state or habit as opposed to just thinking.[1] This group of words occurs often in Philippians—in 1:7; 2:2,5; 3:15,19; and 4:10. In 4:10 it signifies "concern," or focus of attention as well as habit of mind.

For Thought and Discussion: Why do you think people today are so conscious of their rights? Is this good or bad?

Optional Application: How can you put Jesus' mindset toward His rights (see 2:6) into practice?

Nature (2:6-7). "Form" in KJV, NASB, and RSV. As a Greek philosophical term, the word *morphe* means the inward character of a thing as well as the outward expression of that character.[2] It has nothing to do with shape. Light expresses the "form" of fire, and a good deed expresses the "form" of goodness. So, Paul may be saying that Christ both possessed and expressed the essence of deity before His incarnation.[3]

In Jewish literature popular in Paul's day, *morphe* means "condition, status." In this sense, Christ possessed the status and privileges of deity (worthiness of highest honor, lordship) before His incarnation.[4]

2. a. Because He possessed and expressed the essence of Godhead, Jesus had the right to all the worship and lordship the Father had. Yet what was Jesus' mindset toward His rights (see 2:6)?

_____

_____

_____

_____

b. What does this mindset tell you about the humility Paul urges in 2:3? (For instance, how is Jesus' humility different from underrating oneself or feeling worthless?)

_____

_____

_____

_____

_____

_____

_____

Made himself nothing (2:7). Literally, "emptied Himself" (NASB).

3. Other Scriptures stress that Jesus remained fully God while on earth (see Colossians 1:19; 2:9; Hebrews 1:3). Therefore, of what did Jesus empty Himself in becoming human (see Philippians 2:7)?

_____

_____

_____

_____

4. What might Paul mean by saying that Jesus took the form or nature of a *servant* (see 2:7)?

_____

_____

_____

_____

5. The likeness and appearance of a man—human status, feelings, experiences—was humbling enough for Jesus. What was His ultimate humiliation (see 2:8)?

_____

_____

_____

Cross (2:8). Crucifixion was the most degrading execution possible in the Empire. It was the death of a base criminal, never of a Roman citizen. To Jews, a crucified person was clearly accursed by God (see Deuteronomy 21:23; Galatians 3:13).

For Thought and Discussion: Why is it important to understand that Christ is fully human and fully divine?

For Thought and Discussion: If you were God and decided to become human, what would be the hardest part for you?

Optional Application: Why was Jesus willing to be thoroughly humiliated? In what specific ways is this an example you can apply?

For Further Study:
Why was Jesus'
death necessary?
See Leviticus 16:1-22;
2 Corinthians 5:21;
Hebrews 9:26; 1 Peter
2:24; 1 John 4:10.

**For Thought and
Discussion:** What dif-
ference does it make
to our lives that Jesus
is Lord (see 2:11)? (For
example, how should
it move us to respond
to 2:1-8?)

6. How did Jesus exemplify the teaching of
Philippians 2:4 (see 2:7-8)?

_____

_____

_____

_____

_____

Name (2:9). For Jews, the name above every name
was the name of God—YHWH (Yahweh,
Jehovah). God's name was so holy that it was
considered unpronounceable; when reading
Scripture, Jews substituted the word *Lord* for
the name.[5]

---

7. Philippians 2:6-8 tells what Jesus chose to do
in obedience to His Father's will. What did the
Father do in response (see 2:9-11)?

_____

_____

_____

_____

8. The RSV translates 2:5, "Have this mind among
yourselves, which is yours in Christ Jesus."
What does 2:6-11 reveal about the life of a person "in Christ Jesus" (in union with Him and
His church)?

_____

_____

_____

_____

_____

_____

9. Look back at 2:1. What encouragement in
Christ, comfort from His love, and so on, do
you find in 2:6-11?

_____

_____

_____

_____

_____

_____

_____

Study Skill — Application

You may find after a while that application
has become an effort to make yourself better,
and that sheer effort is not making you more
Christlike. When that happens, scale back your
to-do-list, stop watching yourself for failures, and
take more time just thinking about Christ — His
nature, character, deeds, and so on. Ask yourself
if you are relying on God or yourself to enable
you to succeed in your applications (see 1:6).

---

10. Take some time to meditate on 2:5-11.

a. What aspect of Jesus' mindset, the mindset of
a person "in Christ Jesus," would you like to
exercise this week?

_____

_____

_____

_____

_____

_____

b. In what specific ways can you do this?

_____

_____

_____

_____

_____

_____

11. List any questions you have about 2:5-11.

_____

_____

_____

_____

For the group

Worship. Songs of praise for God's love and Christ's work could set the tone for this meeting. Pray that God will lead you beyond intellectual understanding to really see together into His heart.

Summary. Question 1 will remind you of the context of 2:5-11.

Interpretation. The questions in this lesson go through 2:5-11 phrase by phrase, exploring what each phrase means and tying it back to the instructions in 2:1-4. Keep this pattern in mind: (1) What is Paul saying in this verse? (2) What does this have to do with 2:1-4?

Application. Last time, you each named certain areas of your lives on which you wanted to concentrate for growth. You planned to pray for each other, think about Paul's words during the week, look for chances to act obediently, consistently confess and seek forgiveness, and so on. Since 2:5-11 continues the same theme, you might each report briefly on how well you followed through on your commitments and what happened.

For example, one person may have gotten stuck scheduling time to pray, another may have had trouble remembering Paul's words during the day, and another may have noticed for the first time how self-absorbed he really is. This reporting back will update you on how to pray for one another and will allow you to share ideas for how to schedule time, remember during the day, and so on.

After you report back, you can discuss how 2:5-11 motivates each of you to respond. One person may plan to keep pursuing the same mindset she chose last time with the same methods, another may decide to change methods, and another may have found a new insight to focus on.

Summary. Summarize both parts of your discussion: (1) what you learned about God and Christ, and (2) what you learned about how we should act.

Worship. If your discussion has reached above the purely intellectual plane, if you've really seen into the heart of God through this passage, then you will probably be overflowing with thanks and praise for what God has done and the character He has shown.

1. C. G. Moule, *The Epistle to the Philippians* (Grand Rapids, MI: Baker, 1981), 14.
2. James Montgomery Boice, *Philippians: An Expositional Commentary* (Grand Rapids, MI: Zondervan, 1971), 138.
3. Kenneth Wuest, *Philippians in the Greek New Testament* (Grand Rapids, MI: Eerdmans, 1942), 63.
4. Ralph P. Martin, *Philippians* (Grand Rapids, MI: Eerdmans, 1976), 94–98; Kenneth Barker, ed., *The NIV Study Bible* (Grand Rapids, MI: Zondervan, 1985), 1805.
5. Wuest, 71–72; Boice, 149–152.

Lesson Six
PHILIPPIANS 2:12-16
Working It Out

Verses 12 and 13 of chapter 2 have probably sparked
as much debate among Christians as any two verses
in the Bible. The Philippians may have understood
just what Paul meant, for they had learned the
gospel from him directly. For us, the clues to interpretation are the whole mind of Scripture and the
immediate context of what Paul has been talking
about since 1:27.

As you read 2:12-16, ask God to give you insight
into His part and yours in the fulfilling of His "good
work" (see 1:6).

1. What does 2:12-13 have to do with 2:1-11? (The
   word *therefore* is a clue.)

   _____

   _____

   _____

   _____

   _____

   _____

2. How does 2:14-16 further illuminate your
   understanding of 2:12-13?

   _____

   _____

For Further Study:
On our inability to do what we desire without God's enabling, see Romans 7:14–8:10.

For Thought and Discussion: How has God worked in you to will and to act according to His good purpose?

_____

_____

_____

_____

Works in (2:13). "To energize, to work effectively, to provide the necessary power."[1] The same word is translated "do" (KJV), "act" (NIV), or "work" (NASB, RSV) later in the verse.

Will (2:13). To desire, design, intend. Implies choice and purpose.[2]

3. Because we must interpret 2:12 in light of 2:13, we will look at 2:13 first. What does God empower us to will and to do (see 2:13)?

_____

_____

_____

_____

> ### Study Skill — Paraphrasing
> Paraphrasing, putting a passage into your own words, helps you understand it.

4. Restate 2:13 in your own words.

_____

_____

_____

_____

_____

Work out (2:12). "To carry out to the goal, to carry to its ultimate conclusion." [3]

Salvation (2:12). Deliverance from: guilt, our separation from God, a wicked nature, judgment, death, and all other evils. Wholeness, well-being. The Old Testament speaks of salvation and peace as closely connected fruits of the Messianic Age.[4]

5. Because God is empowering us moment by moment, we should continue to work out our salvation with fear and trembling (see 2:12). What does it mean in practice for a Christian to work out his personal salvation? (*Optional*: See Proverbs 3:5-6; Romans 12:1-2; Galatians 5:25; Hebrews 12:1-2.)

_____

_____

_____

_____

_____

_____

_____

_____

_____

_____

For Thought and Discussion:
    a. How is working out your salvation different from working for it?
    b. According to 2:6-11, how did we obtain the "salvation" (2:12) that Paul wants us to work out?
    c. What clues to working out that salvation does 2:1-11 offer?

For Thought and Discussion: What difference should it make to a person's life to know that God is at work in him? How should this affect the way he works out his salvation?

Optional Application: To what extent is your will focused on God's good pleasure? Ask God to work in you to will His purposes in the areas in which you have difficulty doing this.

In 1:27–2:16, Paul stresses the Philippians' partnership. He urges them to contend as one man (see 1:27) and to look to each other's interests (see 2:4). In light of this context, Paul may be exhorting the Philippians to work out their *corporate* salvation (spiritual health, growth in holiness, deliverance from sinful habits) in 2:12.[5] That is, each individual should be trying to help himself, the others, and the group as a whole to grow spiritually.

6. What examples of working out their salvation does Paul give the Philippians in 1:27–2:16?

_____

_____

_____

_____

_____

_____

_____

_____

7. How can a group of Christians help to work out each other's salvation? (*Optional*: See Galatians 6:1-5; Hebrews 3:12-13; 10:24-25; James 5:16,19-20.)

_____

_____

_____

_____

_____

_____

_____

Grumbling (2:14). "Murmurings" (KJV). In the Old Testament, this word describes Israel's discontent with Moses and God during the wilderness wandering. This is not loud dissent, but complaints muttered in small groups.[6]

Arguing (2:14). "Questioning" (RSV), "disputings" (KJV). Disputes out in the open. The word can also mean "litigation."[7]

8. What reasons does Paul give for doing everything without grumbling or arguing (see 2:14-16)?

_____

_____

_____

_____

_____

_____

Blameless . . . pure . . . without fault (2:15). "Not absolute, sinless perfection, but wholehearted, unmixed devotion to doing God's will."[8] (See also the definitions for pure and blameless on pages 29–30.)

---

9. Consider how Paul describes the Christian's mission in the world: shining as "stars" or "lights" and holding out the "word of life" (see 2:15-16). What does this tell you about how we should act?

_____

_____

_____

_____

_____

_____

10. Meditate on one or more of the ways God wants us to work out our salvation (see 1:27–2:16), and on the power God has supplied (see 2:13). Ask God to show you how you could work out your salvation in one of those ways.

a. In what one area would you like to work out your personal salvation?

For Thought and Discussion:
a. What attributes of God do we fail to acknowledge when we grumble or argue?
b. What should we do instead when we don't like what is happening?

For Thought and Discussion: How does not having a grumbling attitude help a person become blameless (see 2:14-15)?

Optional Application: How can you shine as a light and hold out the word of life during the coming week?

For Further Study:
Add 1:27–2:16 to your outline of Philippians, or wait until after lesson 7.

_____

_____

_____

_____

_____

_____

b. What practical steps will you take to do this?

_____

_____

_____

_____

_____

11. Review your answers to questions 6 and 7. How can you help to work out the salvation of your church or fellowship? Try to think of some specific things you could do.

_____

_____

_____

_____

_____

12. List any questions you have about 2:12-16.

_____

_____

_____

_____

For the group

This is a short passage with some crucial teachings in it. The big issues are: (1) What does it mean that God works in us; (2) What does it mean that we must work out our (individual and corporate) salvation; and (3) What does this have to do with Paul's overall topic in 1:27–2:16?

Allow about half your discussion time to explore how you can work out your salvation. You might brainstorm a list of ways, and then let each person who wishes share how he or she plans to apply the teaching. Discuss ways of working out the salvation of your whole group, or of the churches or fellowships you belong to, as well as ways of working out your individual salvation.

Halfway through a study is a good time to evaluate it. Try one of these approaches:

1. Remind the group of the goals you set at the beginning of this study. How well are you meeting them? (For example, in what ways are you getting to know God better? Are you growing more like Christ, and more like partners with each other?) How can you change your meetings to meet those goals better?

2. At the end of your discussion time, you could ask each person to answer three questions briefly:

What did you like best about this meeting?
What did you like least?
How could this study be changed to better meet your needs?

1. Kenneth Wuest, *Philippians in the Greek New Testament* (Grand Rapids, MI: Eerdmans, 1942), 74.
2. W. E. Vine, *An Expository Dictionary of New Testament Words* (Nashville: Royal, 1952), 291, 1229–1230.
3. Wuest, 72; William Barclay, *The Letters to the Philippians, Colossians, and Thessalonians* (Philadelphia: Westminster, 1975), 41.
4. Ralph P. Martin, *Philippians* (Grand Rapids, MI: Eerdmans, 1976), 91–93, 102–103; C. G. Moule, *The Epistle to the Philippians* (Grand Rapids, MI: Baker, 1981), 45; Wuest, 73–74.
5. Martin, 102–103.

6. Wuest, 75; Martin, 104.
7. Wuest, 76; Martin, 104.
8. Kenneth Barker, ed., *The NIV Study Bible* (Grand Rapids, MI: Zondervan, 1985), 1806.

Lesson Seven

PHILIPPIANS 2:17-30

Co-workers

Paul has been urging the Philippians to act in a manner worthy of the gospel (see 1:27) by working humbly and selflessly together. He has motivated them with Christ's example and God's empowering. Now he gives them three other examples of worthy living: himself, Timothy, and Epaphroditus.

Read 2:17-30, noticing how Paul interweaves two purposes—to communicate his plans to send Timothy and Epaphroditus, and to further motivate the Philippians to behave as partners.

Apostle (2:17-18)

Poured out like a drink offering (2:17). In both Roman and Jewish sacrifices, the main offering was an animal killed, and a cup of wine was poured over it as a secondary offering (see Exodus 29:38-41; Numbers 28:6-7).[1]

1. a. What is the main sacrifice Paul mentions in 2:17?

_____

_____

b. What is the secondary offering poured over it?

_____

For Thought and Discussion: Compare 2:17 to 2:7-8. How was Paul following Jesus' example?

Optional Application: Are you joyful while you or someone you love is suffering? Why or why not? Meditate on the convictions that gave Paul joy.

For Thought and Discussion: How many people do you know who are like Timothy? How can you become like him?

c. Paul saw his own suffering and death as secondary to the main sacrifice (see 2:17). How is this attitude a model for us?

_____

_____

_____

_____

_____

2. How was it possible for Paul to be joyful while imprisoned, short of funds, and facing possible death (see 2:17)? What convictions sustained him? (*Optional*: See Philippians 1:12,19-21; Romans 8:18-30; 2 Corinthians 4:13-18.)

_____

_____

_____

_____

_____

_____

Young minister (2:19-24)

Timothy had joined Paul's mission team shortly before it first visited Philippi (see Acts 16:1-12). The colony had given Timothy his first chance to make new disciples, since the team had previously been visiting churches Paul had already founded. Timothy had been with Paul for ten years now, but the people of his first mission field were still dear to him.

Like him (2:20). "Of kindred spirit" in NASB; "like-minded" in KJV. Literally, "of equal soul." Paul may mean that he has no one else so much like

Paul himself, or that he has no one else who so reflects the attitudes he is urging.

3. Compare 2:20-22 to 2:2-4. How does Timothy show the behavior Paul wants the Philippians to have?

verse 20 _____

_____

_____

_____

_____

verse 21 _____

_____

_____

_____

_____

verse 22 _____

_____

_____

_____

_____

4. How could you apply one of Timothy's attitudes toward Paul or the Philippians to the way you work with other Christians?

_____

_____

_____

_____

_____

_____

For Thought and Discussion: In your church or fellowship, what interests do people look out for most (see 2:20-21)?

For Thought and Discussion:
a. What attitudes must a person have if he is to put up with the kind of proving Paul describes in 2:22?
b. Why is this kind of preparation so often necessary for leaders?

For Thought and Discussion: Does Paul imply in 2:26-30 that a Christian should expect perfect health if he is obeying and believing in Jesus? Why or why not?

For Thought and Discussion: What do "fellow worker" and "fellow soldier" mean (see 2:25)? How can we fulfill these roles for other Christians?

Optional Application: Does 2:25,29 suggest any responsibilities you have toward missionaries you or your church support?

Lay person (2:25-30)

5. Observe how Epaphroditus has been working out his own and others' salvation (see 2:25-30). Name three things he has done, and then describe an attitude or quality each action shows.

a. _____

_____

_____

_____

b. _____

_____

_____

_____

c. _____

_____

_____

_____

6. Consider how Paul describes Epaphroditus. What does 2:25 tell you about Christian partnership?

_____

_____

_____

_____

7. Do your circumstances offer you the opportunity to reflect Epaphroditus's qualities in any way? If so, how?

_____

_____

For Further Study:
Add 2:17-30 to your
outline of Philippians,
or outline all of
1:27–2:30.

_____

_____

_____

8. List any questions you have about 2:17-30.

_____

_____

_____

_____

For the group

There isn't much complex theology to unravel
in this passage, just three examples of Christian
living.

Here is one approach to this passage: Make a
list of each thing Paul says about himself, Timothy,
and Epaphroditus. Then interpret and apply each
statement in turn. Explore what the statement
means, and then ask, "How could you/we act in
that way or with that attitude in your/our circumstances?" When you have covered the whole list, let
each person narrow down to one application he or
she wants to focus on during the coming week.

If you have extra time, you could report back
on how past efforts to apply Paul's words are going.
Or, you could review what Paul has said so far and
discuss new ways you've found chapters 1 and 2
relevant to your lives.

Worship. Thank God for the dedication of saints
like Paul, Timothy, and Epaphroditus. Thank Him
for the examples of other saints you know. Ask Him
to reveal to you the interests of Christ Jesus and the
best ways you can serve the welfare of people you
know. Ask Him to work in you to develop the character Paul, Timothy, and Epaphroditus showed.

1. James Montgomery Boice, *Philippians: An Expositional
   Commentary* (Grand Rapids, MI: Zondervan, 1971),
   175–176.

PHILIPPIANS 3:1-11

Gains and Loss

For the most part, the Philippians knew the gospel clearly, and so their task was to work together in accord with their identity "in Christ Jesus" (see 1:27–2:30). But false teachers threatened to undermine the church's firm doctrinal foundation. So, in 3:1-21 Paul reinforced some key doctrines that are at the root of Christian faith and action.

As you read 3:1-11, try to deduce the kinds of errors Paul was refuting. Ask God to show you how a Christian might make similar errors today.

1. What seems to be Paul's overall point in 3:1-11?

_____

_____

_____

_____

Dogs (3:2). One of two kinds of false teachers was trying to mislead the Philippian church. The "dogs" may have been Jewish Christians who wanted Gentile Christians to become full Jews and practice all the Jewish laws. In this case, the teachers were sincere, but sincerely wrong. Or, the "dogs" may have been pretending to uphold Jewish laws with an insincere motive — to avoid persecution from Jews, for example.

**For Thought
and Discussion:**
According to 3:1-11,
why should a
Christian rejoice?
What errors can mis-
lead a Christian so
that he loses his joy?

Circumcision (3:3). A ritual cutting away of the
foreskin, signifying that a man is a Jew (see
Genesis 17:1-14). The cutting represented an
oath that invoked a curse on oneself: it invited
God to cut off the man's life and heirs if he
broke his covenant with God.[1] Circumcision
also demonstrated that a life (the sex organ represented life) was being set apart for God.

    Paul liked to quote Moses' and Jeremiah's
teaching that true circumcision is "circumcision of the heart"—that is, obedience in faith
(see Romans 2:28-29; compare Deuteronomy
10:16; Jeremiah 4:4).

Serve (3:3). "Worship" in KJV: a word normally
used to describe priestly ritual,[2] "the true rite"
of the Lord.

Flesh (3:3). Either the material on which physical
surgeries like circumcision were performed, or
"self"—"man's lower, unredeemed nature, not
inherently bad but the target of sin's attack and
the occasion of his becoming a victim under
sin's dominion."[3] Paul often used the word
"flesh" in this latter sense.

---

2. In 3:3, Paul states four traits of a true Christian.
Choose one of the following two, and explain
what it means.

a. the true circumcision (*Optional*: See Romans
2:28-29; 4:6-12; Galatians 3:7,29; Colossians
2:11-14.)

_____

_____

_____

_____

_____

b. service by the Spirit of God (*Optional*: See
Romans 8:26-27; 12:1; Philippians 2:17;
Hebrews 13:15-16; 1 Peter 2:9.)

_____

_____

_____

_____

_____

_____

Circumcised on the eighth day (3:5). Genesis 17:12 stipulates that sons born to Jewish parents shall be circumcised at eight days of age. Converts, of course, are circumcised when they convert. Paul is saying that he is not just a Jew; he was *born* a Jew. He is no Hellenized Jew; he comes from a Hebrew-speaking family that can trace its lineage to one of the twelve tribes of Israel. Before accepting Christ he had not compromised his Jewish faith by going along with Greek culture; he had scrupulously kept to the strictest of the Jewish schools, the Pharisees. He had obeyed not only the rituals but even the high ethical teachings of Judaism to the utmost of human ability.

3. a. In 3:4-6, Paul explains what it means to "put confidence in the flesh." According to those verses, what sorts of fleshly things could have made Paul feel worthy of God's approval?

_____

_____

_____

_____

_____

b. In what sorts of fleshly things—family history, virtues, talents, and so on—are you tempted to put confidence?

_____

_____

For Further Study:
On boasting in
Christ Jesus, see
1 Corinthians 1:17-25
and 2 Corinthians
12:7-10.

**For Thought and
Discussion:** Why
does the balance
sheet approach to
righteousness endan-
ger a person's joy?

_____

_____

_____

4. Yet, Paul glories not in these things but in
Christ (see 3:3). What does it mean to boast in
Christ Jesus (see 3:7-11)?

_____

_____

_____

_____

_____

_____

_____

Gains . . . loss (3:7-8). Some Jews believed that
God had a sort of balance scale for weighing
good and bad deeds. Some thought that a
person entered heaven if he ended his life with
more on the "gains" side of his good deeds than
on the "loss" side of his wrong doings. The
more good he did, the more were his rewards in
heaven. The idea was similar to an accountant's
balance sheet.[4]

5. Paul says that his virtues and deeds apart from
Christ are not merely *useless* but actually weigh
against him in God's scale (see 3:7-8). Why are
such virtues and deeds worse than useless?
(*Optional*: See John 6:28-29; Romans 10:1-4;
Ephesians 2:10.)

_____

_____

_____

_____

_____

Know (3:10). "To come to know by experience"[5] — personally and intimately, not just from reading or hearing other people's information.

6. For Paul, what is the most valuable thing in life (see 1:21; 3:8)? Use your own words.

_____

_____

_____

_____

_____

Righteousness (3:9). Right relationship to God. For more, see the box, "Righteousness" on page 83.

7. Paul says that his secure standing with God comes "from God" and "through faith in Christ" (3:9). What does this mean? (*Optional*: See Romans 3:19-26.)

_____

_____

_____

_____

_____

_____

Lost all things (3:8). By accepting Christ, Paul gave up his family's affection and inheritance, his community standing, his family's business in Tarsus, and his friends. By becoming a missionary, Paul lost stability, security, sleep, health, wealth, liberty, and eventually life.

For Thought and Discussion: What does it mean to *know* Christ, to *gain* Christ, and to be *found* in Christ?

For Thought and Discussion: How can you tell by looking at a person's life whether Christ is pre-eminent (see 3:8)?

For Thought and Discussion: Think of the person you "know" most intimately. What characteristics make this relationship intimate?

For Thought and Discussion: Does Paul mean that a Christian must literally give up everything for Christ? Why or why not?

Optional Application: What would happen if you considered all things "loss" and "garbage" for Christ's sake? What things might you have to consider loss that you now value? Take some time to write a list of ways this attitude might affect various areas of your life.

8. Make a list of what is valuable (see 1:9-11,18, 23-26; 2:2-4,17) and what is relatively unimport-ant (see 1:12-18,23-24; 3:4-8; 4:11-13) to Paul.

valuable_____

_____

_____

_____

_____

_____

relatively unimportant_____

_____

_____

_____

_____

_____

_____

9. In what ways might adopting Paul's value system affect the way you live?

_____

_____

_____

_____

_____

10. In order to "gain Christ and be found in him" (3:8-9), what does Paul want (see 3:10-11)?

_____

_____

_____

_____

_____

11. Why can't Paul experience Christ's resurrection without sharing in His suffering and death? (*Optional*: See Luke 9:22-26; John 12:23-26; Romans 6:5-10; 2 Corinthians 4:7-18; Hebrews 5:7-9.)

_____

_____

_____

_____

_____

_____

_____

12. How does Philippians show Paul and others identifying with Christ in all aspects of His servanthood, death, and resurrection (see 1:8,12-14,18-30; 2:1-8,17,20-30; 3:4-7,20-21)?

_____

_____

_____

_____

_____

_____

_____

13. What opportunity do you have this week to share in Christ's self-abandonment, submission to God, self-giving, and suffering?

_____

_____

Optional Application: How could you grow to know Christ more intimately?
a. Ask God to nurture in you a desire (see 2:13) to know Christ that outweighs every other desire. Plan to pray about this daily.
b. To know Christ better, meditate daily on 2:6-11 or another passage, such as Colossians 1:15-20 or Isaiah 52:13–53:12.
c. Study Jesus' character in one of the Gospels. Let Philippians 3:10-11 be your motive.
d. What obstacles hinder you from willingly sharing in Christ's sufferings (see Philippians 3:10)? What encourages you to do this? How could you do this more fully this week?

For Thought and Discussion: What can we learn about God's and Christ's nature from 3:1-11?

For Further Study: Outlining an explanation like 3:1-11 can help you trace Paul's train of thought. What is his main point? What are his supporting points?

_____

_____

_____

_____

_____

14. Now that you have studied 3:1-11 more thoroughly, how would you summarize the main point of this passage?

_____

_____

_____

_____

_____

15. List any questions you have about 3:1-11.

_____

_____

_____

_____

For the group

When Paul is making a tight argument, as in 3:1-11, our task is to trace his thought from point to point and grasp his overall message. That is the logic of this lesson.

What is Paul talking about overall (question 1)?
What does he mean in verse 3 (question 2)?
What does he mean by saying that we "put no confidence in the flesh," but rather "boast in Christ Jesus," in verses 3-11 (questions 3–12)?
Again, what is Paul talking about overall (question 14)?
How does all this apply to us (questions 9, 13)?

Be sure to begin and end with a summary of the passage, so that you don't get lost in the details. Use the Optional Applications to spark discussion of application.

Worship. Ask God to show you the things that tempt you to take pride in something other than Christ. Offer to Him any of these things that you can think of. Thank God for making His righteousness available to you. Ask Him to give you intimate knowledge of Christ's power, His sufferings, and Himself. Spend some time just basking in Christ's presence.

Righteousness

The Old Testament called a man righteous if he was living according to the standards of the covenant relationship. This included obedience to God's commands, as well as living "without pride of heart, depending on Yahweh [the LORD] for protection and vindication."[6] However, rabbinic Judaism dropped the part about humble trust in God, and said that righteousness was simply obeying God's commands and doing works of charity and mercy. Jesus (see Matthew 5:20) and Paul (see Philippians 3:9) restored the idea that the purely human righteousness of conformity to the Law would never meet the standards of the covenant relationship. A person must humbly accept God's gift of righteousness.[7]

---

1. Kenneth Barker, ed., *The NIV Study Bible* (Grand Rapids, MI: Zondervan, 1985), 31.
2. C. G. Moule, *The Epistle to the Philippians* (Grand Rapids, MI: Baker, 1981), 58; Kenneth Wuest, *Philippians in the Greek New Testament* (Grand Rapids, MI: Eerdmans, 1942), 88.
3. Ralph P. Martin, *Philippians* (Grand Rapids, MI: Eerdmans, 1976), 126.
4. James Montgomery Boice, *Philippians: An Expositional Commentary* (Grand Rapids, MI: Zondervan, 1971), 193–199; Martin, 129.
5. Wuest, 93.
6. David Hill, *Greek Words and Hebrew Meanings: Studies in the Semantics of Soteriological Terms*, Society for New Testament Studies Monograph Series 5 (Cambridge University, 1967), 92–93.

Lesson Nine

PHILIPPIANS 3:12– 4:1

Citizens of Heaven

In 3:1-11, Paul explains that he takes pride not in who he is by physical birth and what he has done, but in who Christ is and what He has done. Intimately experiencing Christ's power and suffering is Paul's deepest longing. The topic arose because certain people were urging the Philippians to seek security in things other than Christ.

Paul continues this topic through 4:1, explaining why the Philippians should follow his example rather than that of the other teachers. As you read 3:12–4:1, ask God to show you the goal toward which you are pressing.

1. Paul says that he has not already obtained "all this" (3:12; NASB: "it"). What has Paul not obtained (see 3:8-11)?

   _____

   _____

   _____

   _____

2. He goes on to say that he is pressing on to take hold of something. What is "that for which Christ Jesus took hold of me" (see 3:12-14)?

   _____

   _____

For Thought and Discussion: From what you know of Paul's life, how did he press on toward his prize?

Optional Application: What past things do you need to confess, forgive, accept forgiveness for, and forget?

For Thought and Discussion: When Paul speaks of pursuing a prize, is he implying that he is earning something by his work? Why or why not? What point is Paul making in 3:14?

3. a. Paul says he forgets what is behind (see 3:13) as he pursues his prize. What past things might he be forgetting?

_____

_____

_____

_____

_____

_____

b. Why does Paul need to forget these things?

_____

_____

_____

_____

_____

4. Describe one way in which you can forget what lies behind and press on to take hold of the prize God has for you.

_____

_____

_____

_____

_____

Mature (3:15). The same Greek word as "perfect" in verse 12. In verse 12 Paul means that he has not reached such spiritual perfection that he has no further room to grow (and neither have his readers). But in verse 15 he says that those who are relatively perfect—fairly mature with "well rounded Christian character"[1]—should keep in mind that they are still not sinless. As mature as Paul is, he still has a long way to go.

5. Verse 15 suggests that some people in Philippi felt they had attained "sinless perfection."[2]

a. What do you suppose leads some Christians who have reached a certain level of maturity to act as though they have arrived?

_____

_____

_____

_____

_____

b. How can we avoid falling prey to this attitude?

verses 13-14 _____

_____

_____

_____

verse 16 _____

_____

_____

_____

6. a. In 3:18-19 Paul tells us more about the teachers who are trying to mislead the Philippians.[3] For one thing, they are "enemies

For Thought and Discussion:
a. Paul says he will let God deal with those who disagree with him (see 3:15). Why is this often a good response to disagreement?
b. How is this situation different from the one Paul discusses in 1 Timothy 1:3-5?

For Thought and Discussion:
Christians are often full of self-pity and despair when they continue to fail and sin. How is Paul's approach in 3:12-16 different?

For Further Study:
On the centrality of
Jesus' crucifixion, see
1 Corinthians 1:18-25;
Romans 1:16-17;
3:21-26.

of the cross of Christ." In what ways has Paul
been defending Jesus' crucifixion as being
central to the faith (see 2:6-11; 3:3,8-11)?

_____

_____

_____

_____

_____

_____

b. In light of this teaching, how might the false
teachers have been undermining the importance of the Cross?

_____

_____

_____

_____

_____

_____

Their stomach (3:19). If the false teachers were pay-
ing lip service to Jewish rituals, and if they were
claiming to be already perfect, then they may
have been worshiping their stomachs by
(1) making outward rituals like diet the test
of true spiritual maturity and love of God, or
(2) saying that since they were spiritually
mature, they could indulge whatever appetites
they pleased.[4]

7. In what ways might a modern Christian be
tempted to make a god of desires?

_____

_____

_____

_____

_____

_____

_____

Their glory is in their shame (3:19). The false teachers gloried in their circumcision, their possession of the Holy Spirit, and their spiritual maturity (see 3:2-3,12,15), rather than in the atoning death of Jesus. However, even wonderful things like these would be "garbage" in Paul's eyes (see 3:7-8) if they hindered a person from humbly receiving God's mercy. Anything that prevented boasting (see 3:3) in Christ would lead to destruction and shame.[5]

8. Rather than on earthly lineage, wealth, education, rituals, or virtue, what is Paul's mind focused on (see 3:20-21)?

_____

_____

_____

_____

Citizenship (3:20). _Politeuma_ is a word akin to the manner of conduct in 1:27 (see the note on manner on pages 43–44). Again, Paul is speaking to people who treat the privileges and duties of Roman citizenship with great seriousness.

9. Think about the fact that you are a citizen of heaven. What differences should this fact make to your outlook, behavior, and priorities?

_____

_____

For Further Study:
a. On our citizenship in heaven, see John 17:14-16; 1 Corinthians 7:29-31; 2 Corinthians 5:18-21; 1 Peter 2:11.
b. On our bodily transformation, see 1 Corinthians 15:12-58.

Optional Application: Meditate on your expectation of having a body as glorious as Jesus' (see 3:21). How does this expectation help you to deal with your current body?

For Further Study:
Add 3:12–4:1 to your outline.

_____

_____

_____

_____

10. Paul sums up 3:1-21 by saying, "Therefore, . . . stand firm in the Lord in this way" (4:1). How would you summarize the way we should stand firm, according to chapter 3?

_____

_____

_____

_____

11. What to you is the most important insight you found in 3:12–4:1? Write it down, along with at least one implication it has for your life.

_____

_____

_____

_____

_____

_____

12. List any questions you have about this passage.

_____

_____

_____

_____

Crown (4:1). Not the Greek word for a king's crown. Rather, this is the crown awarded to a victorious athlete, or the crown with which guests were crowned at a joyful banquet.[6]

For the group

Orienting. After opening in prayer or worship, you can do some things to help orient anyone who has lost track of Paul's topic during a busy week. Have someone read 3:12–4:1 aloud, then ask someone to summarize what Paul said in 3:1-11, and finally ask someone to summarize 3:12–4:1.

Restating. In even the best study guide, a question is occasionally unclear. Also, groups often find it helpful and more interesting when leaders rephrase the questions instead of just repeating them. So, when you want to restate a question, keep these two sets of categories in mind: (1) the procedure of observe-interpret-apply; and (2) the topics of "Who is God?" "Who am I?" and "What should I do?"

For example, you can restate an observation question like this: "What does this verse (or paragraph) say about God or Christ (His character, acts, and so on)?" Or, "What does this verse (or paragraph) say about man's unredeemed nature or his nature/identity in Christ?" Or, "What does this paragraph say we should think or do because we are in Christ?"

For interpretation questions, you can ask, "What does the phrase '. . .' mean?" Or, "What is Paul trying to tell us about God (or Christ, or man, or what we should do)?"

For application questions, try asking, "How does this passage apply to you?" Or, "What implications does this passage have for your life?"

Worship. Take some silent time together to think about your current citizenship and future goal in heaven. Then begin to thank God for these gifts. Ask Him to keep you aware of them during the coming week. Ask Him to enable you to press on toward the goal and to forget what is behind.

For Thought and Discussion:
a. Why were the Philippians Paul's crown of victory and celebration?
b. What people or things, if any, give you a sense of joy and victory? Why is this so? How can you shape your life so that other Christians become your joy and crown?

1. Kenneth Wuest, *Philippians in the Greek New Testament* (Grand Rapids, MI: Eerdmans, 1942), 99.
2. Wuest, 100.
3. Some commentators believe that the people described in Philippians 3:18-19 were different from those refuted in Philippians 3:2-11. It is hard to know for certain the circumstances behind this chapter since Paul merely alludes to a situation that he and the Philippians already understand. Ralph P. Martin, *Philippians* (Grand Rapids, MI: Eerdmans, 1976), 22–36, explains many possible reconstructions of the situation in Philippi.
4. Martin, 22–34, 145; Wuest, 101.
5. Martin, 145–146.
6. William Barclay, *The Letters to the Philippians, Colossians, and Thessalonians* (Philadelphia: Westminster, 1975), 70.

Lesson Ten

PHILIPPIANS 4:2-23

The Peace of God

Exhortations (4:2-9)

As he moves toward a closing, Paul lists a series of exhortations in 4:2-9. After you read the passage, you might list each instruction mentally or on paper.

___

Be of the same mind (4:2). The same expression as the one in 2:2 rendered "being like-minded."

Companion (4:3). In KJV, "yokefellow" is used, which could be a name (Syzygus) or a term to describe one of the Philippians. It is possible that someone took the name Syzygus at baptism, a Christian name to replace his pagan one and to symbolize his new birth.

___

1. According to 4:2-3, how does Paul want some of the Philippians to put into practice his teachings from 1:27–2:18? Explain his counsel in your own words.

   Euodia and Syntyche _____

   _____

   _____

   _____

For Thought and Discussion: Does being of the same mind "in the Lord" (4:2) mean that we must come to the same opinions? If so, why? If not, what does it mean?

For Thought and Discussion:
   a. What does it mean to rejoice "in the Lord" (4:4)?
   b. Why should we do this?
   c. What other things do people rejoice in, besides union with Christ?

For Thought and Discussion: In 4:5, Paul links the fact that "the Lord is near" with an exhortation to manifest gentleness. Why should this fact lead us to be gentle?

For Thought and Discussion:
a. How have you been treated with gentleness in the past?

b. Do you prefer to be treated with strict fairness or gentleness? Do you tend to treat people justly or gently? What are the advantages and disadvantages of each approach?

Optional Application:
a. What chances might you have to show gentleness to someone during the coming week?

b. For one day, look for opportunities to be gentle. Try to write down or make a mental note of each opportunity.

the "true companion" _____

_____

_____

_____

Gentleness (4:5). "Moderation" in KJV; "forbearance" in RSV. "Not being unduly rigorous, being satisfied with less than one's due."[1] "Graciousness, . . . willingness to forgo retaliation when Christians are threatened or provoked."[2]

A gentle person "will rather take sides against himself, look from the other's point of view, remember his own duties and the other's rights." He "will yield like air in matters of personal feeling or interest," but "will stand like rock in respect of moral principle."[3]

---

2. Give an example from your own experience when strict justice demanded that you treat someone in one way, but gentleness demanded that you respond differently.

_____

_____

_____

_____

_____

Anxious (4:6). "Self-centered, counterproductive worry, not legitmate cares and concerns . . ."[4]

3. What should a Christian do when he or she has a need (see 4:6)?

_____

_____

_____

_____

_____

4. Does Paul guarantee that you will get what you ask (see 4:7,12-13)?

_____

_____

_____

5. Why is it important for us to focus our minds on true and excellent things (see 4:8)? (See also 2 Corinthians 10:4-5; Philippians 1:10; Colossians 3:1-3.)

_____

_____

_____

_____

6. Thinking rightly is important (see 4:8). Still, what higher standard does Paul give for Christians (see 4:9)?

_____

_____

_____

Thanks for sharing (4:10-20)

Last of all, Paul comes to the immediate occasion of his letter—thanks for the gift of money that the Philippians had sent to support him in prison. As always, he makes use of a chance to teach proper attitudes in the midst of his thanks.

Optional Application: Make a list of all the things you are anxious about. Consciously offer each one to the Lord, thanking Him for supplying you with peace and all other needs. Spend some time in thanksgiving about each matter.

For Thought and Discussion:
a. Why does a Christian not have to be anxious about his needs (see 4:6-7,11-13,19)?
b. Why should thanksgiving accompany our prayers (see 4:6-7)?

Optional Application: Recall the meaning of "peace" from 1:2 on page 26. Meditate on the peace of God and the God of peace (see 4:7,9).

For Thought and Discussion: Give some examples of things that are true, noble, and so on (see 4:8).

For Thought and Discussion: Why does Paul give his own teaching and example as the model for Christian action?

Optional Application: For one full day, try to be aware of what you think about during free moments. Practice consciously shifting your thoughts to something true, or noble, or right, or praiseworthy.

For Thought and Discussion: What implications, if any, does 4:8 have for a Christian's attitude toward the arts, habits of television and film viewing, reading matter, other pastimes?

Optional Application: Meditate on what Paul has learned (see 4:11-13). What implications does it have for the way you use your thoughts and energy?

For Thought and Discussion: What resources is Paul content with (see 4:13)? Could you be content with those?

Content (4:11). Sufficient, complete, satisfied with one's resources.

7. Paul says he rejoices in the Philippians' concern, but not because he is in need. Why doesn't physical need worry Paul (see 4:11-13)?

_____

_____

_____

_____

_____

8. How has Paul learned to be content? (See 2 Corinthians 1:8-10; 11:23-28; 12:8-10; 1 Timothy 6:6-8.)

_____

_____

_____

_____

_____

_____

_____

9. If Paul is content, then why do the Philippians' concern and giving make him joyful (see 4:17-19)?

_____

_____

_____

_____

_____

10. What does 4:14-16 add to your understanding of Christian partnership/fellowship?

_____

_____

_____

_____

_____

_____

11. How does God respond when we make offerings to Him by giving to others (see 4:18-19)?

_____

_____

_____

_____

12. How would you summarize the main message Paul wants to get across in 4:2-20?

_____

_____

_____

_____

_____

13. a. What seems most significant to you of all that Paul says in 4:2-20?

_____

_____

_____

_____

_____

For Thought and Discussion: What is the connection between 4:6-7 and 4:11-13?

Optional Application: Could you be a partner with another Christian in ministry, as the Philippians were partners with Paul? How could you go about choosing a partner and finding out how best to support him or her?

For Thought and Discussion: In what sense is the Philippians' gift to Paul an offering to God (see 4:18)?

Optional Application: What might it mean for you to "stand firm in the Lord" (4:1), "be of the same mind in the Lord" (4:2), or "rejoice in the Lord" (4:4) this week?

For Further Study:
Add 4:2-23 to your
outline of Philippians.

b. What is one implication this truth has for
   your life?

_____

_____

_____

_____

_____

_____

_____

c. Paul tells us to *practice* what he says (see 4:9).
   How might you put into practice one thing he
   says in 4:2-20 during the coming week?

_____

_____

_____

_____

_____

_____

Caesar's household (4:22). "Not blood relatives
   of the emperor, but those employed (slaves or
   freedmen) in or around the palace area (compare 'palace guard,' 1:13)."[5]

14. List any questions you have about 4:2-23.

_____

_____

_____

_____

For the group

You may decide to touch lightly on each issue this passage raises or to explore one or two more thoroughly. The main issues are: (1) being of the same mind "in the Lord" and helping one another do this; (2) gentleness; (3) thankful prayer instead of anxiety; (4) what to think about and what to practice; (5) contentedness in all circumstances; and (6) the partnership of sharing funds.

You can practice Paul's teaching as a group in lots of ways. You can be of the same mind in the Lord, rejoice in the Lord together, treat each other with gentleness, present your requests to God with thanks, and even become partners together with the missionary or other Christian worker of your choice. Which of these applications suit your group?

The final lesson in this study is a review of the whole book of Philippians. The review asks you to reread the letter, pull together its teaching on various themes, and outline the letter. The outline will be somewhat easier because you have already summarized each passage. However, you might advise the group that if time constrains anyone to omit any part of the review, then he or she should omit the outline. It is less important than rereading the book, pulling the themes together, and thinking about past and future application.

Worship.

1. Kenneth Wuest, *Philippians in the Greek New Testament* (Grand Rapids, MI: Eerdmans, 1942), 109.
2. Ralph P. Martin, *Philippians* (Grand Rapids, MI: Eerdmans, 1976), 154–155.
3. C. G. Moule, *The Epistle to the Philippians* (Grand Rapids, MI: Baker, 1981), 80.
4. Kenneth Barker, ed., *The NIV Study Bible* (Grand Rapids, MI: Zondervan, 2002), 1848.
5. Barker, 1810.

Lesson Eleven

REVIEW

Now that you've studied Philippians in detail, do you have a firm grasp of the book as a whole? If your head is full of a jumble of details and individual verses, a review can help you sort out what you've learned.

1. First, reread all of Philippians. It should be familiar by now, so you should be able to read rapidly, looking for threads that tie the letter together. Pray for a fresh perspective on what God is saying. Don't get bogged down; just do what you can with the time God has given you.

2. In lesson 1, question 4, you were asked what you thought Paul's aims for this letter were. After closer study, how would you now explain his purposes?

_____

_____

_____

_____

_____

_____

3. (*Optional*) With those purposes in mind, make up a brief outline of Philippians. (You may

find it helpful to review your titles and your summaries of passages on page 30 (question 8), page 35 (question 1), page 38 (question 7), page 46 (question 4), page 53 (question 1), page 61 (question 1), page 75 (question 1), page 90 (question 10), and page 97 (question 12).

I. (1:1-2) _____

II. (1:3-11) _____

_____

III. (1:12-26) _____

_____

IV. (1:27–2:18) _____

_____

_____

_____

_____

_____

_____

V. (2:19-30) _____

_____

_____

_____

VI. (3:1–4:1) _____

_____

_____

_____

_____

_____

VII. (4:2-23) _____

_____

_____

_____

_____

_____

_____

_____

4. What are the most important lessons you
learned from Philippians about the following
topics? (Some sample verses are given to help
you, but you may benefit more from skimming
the whole letter.)

partnership in Christ (see 1:4-11,24-30;
2:1-4,17-30; 3:10-11,17; 4:1-3,10,14-19)

_____

_____

_____

_____

_____

joy (see 1:4,18-19,25-26; 2:2,17-18,29-30; 3:1;
4:1,4,10)

_____

_____

_____

_____

_____

circumstances and suffering (see 1:12-26; 4:11-13)

_____

_____

_____

_____

_____

Christ (see 1:6,11,20-26,29; 2:5-11; 3:3-11)

_____

_____

_____

_____

_____

the Christian mind (see 2:2,5,13,20-21; 3:19-20; 4:2,7-8)

_____

_____

_____

_____

knowledge and knowing (see 1:9,12,16,19,22,25, 27; 3:8,10; 4:12,15)

_____

_____

_____

_____

_____

_____

courage and confidence (see 1:6,14,20,27-28; 2:1; 3:3-7; 4:6)

_____

_____

_____

_____

_____

_____

God at work in us (see 1:6; 2:13; 3:12,14,21; 4:7,13)

_____

_____

_____

_____

_____

_____

other _____

_____

_____

_____

_____

_____

5. Review the questions you listed at the ends of lessons 1 through 10. Do any questions that seem important to you remain unanswered? If so, some of the sources in Study Aids on pages 111–115 may help you answer some of your questions. Or, you might study some particular passage with cross-references on your own.

For Further Study: Choose one key verse that expresses for you the essence of Philippians. Memorize that verse.

6. Have you noticed any areas (thoughts, attitudes, opinions, behavior) in which you have changed as a result of studying Philippians? If so, how have you changed?

_____

_____

_____

_____

_____

_____

7. Look back over the entire study at questions in which you expressed a desire to make some specific application. Are you satisfied with your follow-through? Pray about any of those areas that you think you should continue to pursue specifically.

What topic (or topics) from Philippians continues to challenge you personally, and what do you plan to do about it?

_____

_____

_____

_____

_____

_____

_____

For the group

Reading aloud. It might take fifteen minutes to read the whole book of Philippians aloud. You would probably find this helpful in refreshing everyone's memory. However, if you prefer to save time, try having a different person summarize each passage in the letter.

Purpose and outline. A review of the main goals of the letter (question 2) would be especially worthwhile. However, you might warn the group before preparing for your meeting that some people find that outlining takes a lot of time. In order to allow plenty of time to prepare and discuss question 4, you might want to treat question 3 as a helpful option. Advise anyone under time constraints to skip question 3 rather than another question.

Themes. This should be the heart of your discussion. Try combining questions 4, 6, and 7 as follows.

Consider the first theme—partnership/fellowship. Take about five minutes to recall everything Paul says about it, and then turn to application. Let group members share how Paul's teaching on fellowship has affected their attitudes about other Christians, perspectives on their own mission, and actions. Then ask if anyone has plans to pursue further action in response to Paul's teaching on partnership.

Then treat the next theme—joy—in the same way, and so on through the list. Skip any of the items you all agree to skip, in the interest of time.

Questions. Be sure to allow time for group members to raise questions that remain unanswered (question 5). As a general rule, the group leader should never do what the group can do for itself, so it would be better to direct people to sources where they can find answers than to just answer their questions. Better still, let the group answer an individual's questions, based on what you have all learned from studying Philippians.

Evaluation. Take a few minutes or a whole meeting to evaluate how your group functioned during your study of Philippians. Some questions you might ask are:

How well did the study help you grasp
    Philippians?
What were the most important truths you discovered together about the Lord?
What did you like best about your meetings?
What did you like least? What would you change?

How well did you meet the goals you set at your
   first meeting?
What did you learn about small-group study?
What are members' current needs and interests?
   What will you do next?

Worship. Thank God for specific things He has
taught you and specific ways He has changed you
through Philippians. Thank Him also for the opportunity to study the Bible together. Ask Him to guide
you as to what to do next.

GOING ON IN PHILIPPIANS

Ideas for Further Study

1. Any of the topics listed for lesson 11, question 4 would be ideal for topical study. Begin by going back through each reference in Philippians and writing down what you learn. You could take weeks just meditating on and applying those references. Then, use a concordance or a Bible with cross-references to find other references to those topics.

2. As in Paul's day, there is a lot of false teaching circulating today. How would Paul counter the teaching that . . .

   a Christian can reach perfect sanctification (holiness) in this life (see 3:12-16)?

   our resurrection is merely spiritual new life, or an immortal soul (see 3:10-11,20-21)?

   a Christian should focus on working out his own salvation (growing spiritually himself) and be less concerned about other people's spiritual growth (see 2:1-13)?

   a truly mature, faithful Christian will be happy, prosperous, and healthy (see 1:12-13,29-30; 2:5-11,29-30; 3:10-11; 4:12-13)? Is suffering part of the Christian life? Why or why not?

   it doesn't matter what a Christian does, as long as he believes in Christ (see 1:27; 2:12-13; 3:12-14,17-21)?

   God won't love you unless you do your very best to do right (see 2:6-11; 3:2-11)?

   the kingdom of God is here and now, so it is escapist to focus on future salvation (see 1:20-24; 3:10-11,20-21)?

   the kingdom of God is in the future, so it is worldly to care about what happens here (see 1:20-30; 2:29-30; 4:14-17)?

3. List all the verses in Philippians that imply effort on our part, and all those that imply effort on God's part. Then summarize our responsibility and His. (For instance, see 1:6; 2:12-13; 3:12-14; 4:13.)

STUDY AIDS

For further information on the material covered in this study, consider the following sources. If your local bookstore does not have them, you can ask the bookstore to order them from the publishers, or find them in a public university or seminary library. If they are out of print, you might be able to find them online.

Commentaries on Philippians

Boice, James Montgomery. *Philippians: An Expositional Commentary* (Zondervan, 1971).
　　This book is based on a series of Boice's sermons and emphasizes what Paul's words mean for modern people. Boice helps the reader to understand and identify with what was going on in Paul's and the Philippians' lives, and shows how Paul's teaching applies today.

Martin, Ralph. *Philippians* (Eerdmans, 1976).
　　A fine best choice if you want a straight verse-by-verse commentary on what the text means. Martin explains words well and gives clear, non-technical discussions of various interpretations of difficult passages.

Wiersbe, Warren. *Be Joyful* (Victor, 1974).
　　Wiersbe shows how each section of Philippians teaches us to be joyful Christians, despite people and circumstances, by putting God and other people ahead of ourselves. Wiersbe's illustrations help the reader to apply the text, and his outline of the book is easy to remember.

Historical sources

Bruce, F. F. *New Testament History* (Doubleday, 1979).
　　A history of Herodian kings, Roman governors, philosophical schools, Jewish sects, Jesus, the early Jerusalem church, Paul, and early Gentile Christianity. Well-documented with footnotes for the serious student, but the notes do not intrude.

Bruce, F. F. *Paul, Apostle of the Heart Set Free* (Eerdmans, 1977).
Possibly the best book around on the historical background and
chronology of Paul's life. Bruce explains Paul's personality and thought
from an evangelical perspective, although some readers will disagree
with his interpretation at points.

Harrison, E. F. *Introduction to the New Testament* (Eerdmans, 1971).
History from Alexander the Great—who made Greek culture domi-
nant in the biblical world—through philosophies, pagan and Jewish
religions, Jesus' ministry and teaching (the book's weakest section), and
the spread of Christianity. Very good maps and photographs of the land,
art, and architecture of New Testament times.

Histories, concordances, dictionaries, and handbooks

A **history** or **survey** traces Israel's history from beginning to end, so that
you can see where each biblical event fits. *A Survey of Israel's History* by
Leon Wood (Zondervan, 1970) is a good basic introduction for lay people
from a conservative viewpoint. Not critical or heavily learned, but not sim-
plistic. Many other good surveys are also available. On the Persian period,
serious students will enjoy *History of the Persian Empire* by A. T. Olmstead
(University of Chicago, 1948). Also, Herodotus's *Histories* is available in an
English translation from several publishers.

A **concordance** lists words of the Bible alphabetically along with each verse in
which the word appears. It lets you do your own word studies. An *exhaustive*
concordance lists every word used in a given translation, while an *abridged*
or *complete concordance* omits either some words, some occurrences of the
word, or both.
Two of the three best exhaustive concordances are the venerable
Strong's Exhaustive Concordance and *Young's Analytical Concordance to
the Bible*. Both are available based on the King James Version and the New
American Standard Bible. *Strong's* has an index in which you can find out
which Greek or Hebrew word is used in a given English verse (although
its information is occasionally outdated). *Young's* breaks up each English
word it translates. Neither concordance requires knowledge of the original
languages.
Perhaps the best exhaustive concordance currently on the market is *The
NIV Exhaustive Concordance*. It features a Hebrew-to-English and a Greek-
to-English lexicon (based on the eclectic text underlying the NIV), which are
also keyed to *Strong's* numbering system.
Among other good, less expensive concordances, *Cruden's Complete
Concordance* is keyed to the King James and Revised Versions, and the *NIV
Complete Concordance* is keyed to the New International Version. These
include all references to every word included, but they omit "minor" words.
They also lack indexes to the original languages.

A **Bible dictionary** or **Bible encyclopedia** alphabetically lists articles about people, places, doctrines, important words, customs, and geography of the Bible.

The New Bible Dictionary edited by J. D. Douglas, F. F. Bruce, J. I. Packer, N. Hillyer, D. Guthrie, A. R. Millard, and D. J. Wiseman (Tyndale, 1982) is more comprehensive than most dictionaries. Its 1,300 pages include quantities of information along with excellent maps, charts, diagrams, and an index for cross-referencing.

Unger's Bible Dictionary by Merrill F. Unger (Moody, 1979) is equally good and is available in an inexpensive paperback edition.

The Zondervan Pictorial Encyclopedia edited by Merrill C. Tenney (Zondervan, 1975, 1976) is excellent and exhaustive, and has been revised and updated. Its five 1,000-page volumes represent a significant financial investment, however, and all but very serious students may prefer to use it at a church, public college, or seminary library.

Unlike a Bible dictionary in the above sense, *Vine's Expository Dictionary of New Testament Words* by W. E. Vine (various publishers) alphabetically lists major words used in the King James Version and defines each New Testament Greek word that the KJV translates with its English word. *Vine's* also lists verse references where that Greek word appears, so you can do your own cross-references and word studies without knowing any Greek.

Vine's is a good, basic book for beginners, but it is much less complete than other Greek helps for English speakers. More serious students might prefer *The New International Dictionary of New Testament Theology* edited by Colin Brown (Zondervan) or *The Theological Dictionary of the New Testament* by Gerhard Kittel and Gerhard Friedrich, abridged in one volume by Geoffrey W. Bromiley (Eerdmans).

A **Bible atlas** can be a great aid to understanding what is going on in a book of the Bible and how geography affected events. Here are a few good choices.

The MacMillan Atlas by Yohanan Aharoni and Michael Avi-Yonah (MacMillan, 1968, 1977) contains 264 maps, 89 photos, and 12 graphics. The many maps of individual events portray battles, movements of people, and changes of boundaries in detail.

The New Bible Atlas by J. J. Bimson and J. P. Kane (Tyndale, 1985) has 73 maps, 34 photos, and 34 graphics. Its evangelical perspective, concise and helpful text, and excellent research make it a very good choice, but its greatest strength lies in outstanding graphics, such as cross-sections of the Dead Sea.

The Bible Mapbook by Simon Jenkins (Lion, 1984) is much shorter and less expensive than most other atlases, so it offers a good first taste of the usefulness of maps. It contains 91 simple maps, very little text, and 20 graphics. Some of the graphics are computer-generated and intriguing.

The Moody Atlas of Bible Lands by Barry J. Beitzel (Moody, 1984) is scholarly, evangelical, and full of theological text, indexes, and references. This admirable reference work will be too deep and costly for some, but Beitzel shows vividly how God prepared the land of Israel perfectly for the acts of salvation He planned to accomplish in it.

A **handbook** of biblical customs can also be useful. Some good ones are *Today's Handbook of Bible Times and Customs* by William L. Coleman (Bethany, 1984) and the less detailed *Daily Life in Bible Times* (Nelson, 1982).

For small-group leaders

Barker, Steve, et al. *The Small Group Leader's Handbook* (InterVarsity, 1982).
> Written by an InterVarsity small group with college students primarily in mind. It includes information on small-group dynamics and how to lead in light of them, and many ideas for worship, building community, and outreach. It has a good chapter on doing inductive Bible study.

Griffin, Em. *Getting Together: A Guide for Good Groups* (InterVarsity, 1982).
> Applies to all kinds of groups, not just Bible studies. From his own experience, Griffin draws deep insights into why people join groups; how people relate to each other; and principles of leadership, decision making, and discussions. It is fun to read, but its 229 pages will take more time than the above book.

Hunt, Gladys. *You Can Start a Bible Study Group* (Harold Shaw, 1984).
> Builds on Hunt's thirty years of experience leading groups. This book is wonderfully focused on God's enabling. It is both clear and applicable for Bible study groups of all kinds.

McBride, Neal F. *How to Build a Small Groups Ministry* (NavPress, 1994).
> This hands-on workbook for pastors and lay leaders includes everything you need to know to develop a plan that fits your unique church. Through basic principles, case studies, and worksheets, McBride leads you through twelve logical steps for organizing and administering a small-groups ministry.

McBride, Neal F. *How to Lead Small Groups* (NavPress, 1990).
> Covers leadership skills for all kinds of small groups — Bible study, fellowship, task, and support groups. Filled with step-by-step guidance and practical exercises to help you grasp the critical aspects of small-group leadership and dynamics.

Bible study methods

Braga, James. *How to Study the Bible* (Multnomah, 1982).
> Clear chapters on a variety of approaches to Bible study: synthetic, geographical, cultural, historical, doctrinal, practical, and so on. Designed to help the ordinary person without seminary training to use these approaches.

Fee, Gordon, and Douglas Stuart. *How to Read the Bible for All Its Worth* (Zondervan, 1982).

After explaining in general what interpretation and application are, Fee and Stuart offer chapters on interpreting and applying the different kinds of writing in the Bible: Epistles, Gospels, Old Testament Law, Old Testament narrative, the Prophets, Psalms, Wisdom, and Revelation. Fee and Stuart also suggest good commentaries on each biblical book. They write as evangelical scholars who personally recognize Scripture as God's Word for their daily lives.

Jensen, Irving L. *Independent Bible Study* (Moody, 1963), and *Enjoy Your Bible* (Moody, 1962).

The former is a comprehensive introduction to the inductive Bible study method, especially the use of synthetic charts. The latter is a simpler introduction to the subject.

Wald, Oletta. *The Joy of Discovery in Bible Study* (Augsburg, 1975).

Wald focuses on issues such as how to observe all that is in a text, how to ask questions of a text, how to use grammar and passage structure to see the writer's point, and so on. Very helpful on these subjects.

Encounter God's Word

EXPERIENCE LIFECHANGE

FROM THE NAVIGATORS

THE LIFECHANGE BIBLE STUDY SERIES

can help you grow in Christlikeness through a life-changing
encounter with God's Word. Discover what the Bible says and
develop the skills and desire to dig even deeper into Scripture.
Each study includes study aids and discussion questions.

AVAILABLE AT NAVPRESS.COM
OR WHEREVER BOOKS ARE SOLD.

SINGLE COPIES AND BULK DISCOUNTS AT NAVPRESS.COM

CP1212

THE NAVIGATORS® STORY

———— ◐ ————

THANK YOU for picking up this NavPress book! I hope it has been a blessing to you.

NavPress is a ministry of The Navigators. The Navigators began in the 1930s, when a young California lumberyard worker named Dawson Trotman was impacted by basic discipleship principles and felt called to teach those principles to others. He saw this mission as an echo of 2 Timothy 2:2: "And the things you have heard me say in the presence of many witnesses entrust to reliable people who will also be qualified to teach others" (NIV).

In 1933, Trotman and his friends began discipling members of the US Navy. By the end of World War II, thousands of men on ships and bases around the world were learning the principles of spiritual multiplication by the person-to-person teaching of God's Word.

After World War II, The Navigators expanded its ministry to include college campuses; local churches; the Glen Eyrie Conference Center and Eagle Lake Camps in Colorado Springs, Colorado; and neighborhood and citywide initiatives across the country and around the world.

Today, with more than 2,600 US staff members—and local ministries in more than 100 countries—The Navigators continue the process of making disciples who make more disciples, advancing the Kingdom of God in a world that desperately needs the hope and salvation of Jesus Christ and the encouragement to grow deeper in relationship with Him.

NAVPRESS was created in 1975 to advance the calling of The Navigators by bringing biblically rooted and culturally relevant products to people who want to know and love Christ more deeply. In January 2014, NavPress entered into an alliance with Tyndale House Publishers to strengthen and better position our rich content for the future. Through *The Message* Bible and other resources, NavPress seeks to bring positive spiritual movement to people's lives.

If you're interested in learning more or becoming involved with The Navigators, go to www.navigators.org. For more discipleship content from The Navigators and NavPress authors, visit www.thedisciplemaker.org. May God bless you in your walk with Him!

Sincerely,

DON PAPE
VP/PUBLISHER, NAVPRESS

www.navpress.com

CP1308